My Nanny Is A Lesbian

Rugie Callas

Acknowledgements

The person that needs to be acknowledged for helping me write this is first and foremost, Josefina C., who interviewed me and sparked the idea of writing my memoir. If it had not been for her, I never would have taken on this huge challenge.

Next, I want to thank Sylvan Warner and Mahria who helped edit this work.

I also want to thank my grandson, Zachary Douglas, who was the first person who laughed and said he loved what I was writing. He encouraged me to continue and through his heartfelt laughter made me realize I could connect to people through my writing.

And the person who made the completion of this work possible is my dear friend, who is like a granddaughter to me, Karen Valenzuela. I cannot believe that I am finally publishing. It has to be one of the many miracles of my life thanks to Karen and everyone else's dedicated work.

I am thankful for the many memoir classes I have taken over the years with all the people that have enjoyed my memoir and helped me realize I should publish this.

I want to thank everybody from the bottom of my heart.

"My life is Nam-myoho-renge-kyo; I am a Buddha; I am living as a Bodhisattva of the Earth; therefore, I can bring this power out and solve my problem. Not only do I deserve to be happy, I must become happy; that's how I will demonstrate the Great Law."

Table of Contents

Chapter 1, My Nanny Is A Lesbian

When my grandson, Miles, introduced me to his classmates in the fifth grade, he stood up and said, "This is my nanny. She's a lesbian." The class howled with laughter. The memory of that day lingered. The pride with which he introduced me made me feel like he really captured my essence. I knew one day it would be a great title for a memoir. It just sounded right. Many years later, after being interviewed by a friend and responding to her comment, "This is fascinating, you should write that down," I picked up a pen to finally begin writing my story.

I was born in 1936 in San Francisco at the height of the Great Depression. I must have known it was not safe to come into the tumultuous world of my parent's marriage. I put my mother through a difficult time resisting birth and entering the world feet first. This would be symbolic of my life of running, running and never stopping until I hit my 70s.

I arrived in the wee hours of the morning to parents who were both in love with other people. My older sister, Dottie, and I were both unwanted as females. My parents wanted boys and maybe that's why I wanted to be one all my life.

Ours was a house of silence except for my father's rage filled outbursts. The house was devoid of love and filled with neglect. My mother suffered an accident when I was three weeks old: a water heater blew up and scarred her entire upper chest. She wore an impenetrable plaster cast making it difficult for her to hold or care for me. She was in bed for months and I have no memory of anyone providing for my needs. As a child I learned I had to take care of myself, and this is what I have been doing my entire life. Growing up, I was never acknowledged and I wasn't appreciated, I was given orders as to what I needed to do. Did I even exist?

Although I was neglected, I was given strict boundaries to obey. I impulsively tested them on occasion. One of my first memories, at age three, is a perfect example. My mother had told me not to go downstairs to the basement where my father rebuilt cars that had been in accidents. I saw a big shiny black car. I was curious and when I climbed into the back seat, I saw a woman's white leather sandal covered in blood. The seat was also stained with blood. My imagination immediately took me to the scene of the crime where someone had crashed into this big, beautiful car with long running boards. I always wondered if the woman had died in that accident.

After I crept up the basement stairs and went back to my bed, I had nightmares of cars crashing and people getting killed. The intensity of my nightmares taught me why my mother told me not to go downstairs. I avoided the basement from then on.

Chapter 2, My Early Years

Mill Valley, a small town in Marin county, became our next home in 1938. I was two years old at the time. My mom had always looked very sad; she wore worry daily in her eyes until that glorious day of my brother George's arrival from the hospital. It was October 1st, 1940 when she finally had the boy she always wanted. Up to that point, it seemed she lived in her own private, silent world where I could never go. To see her finally smile thrilled me. I shall never forget that moment, it was a moment frozen in time. I thought we were finally going to be a happy family. Dad was wrestling with my sister and I on the floor when all of a sudden Mom entered the house with a huge smile on her face and full of joy carrying her first son. It was as if the birth of her son gave birth to a part of herself I had never seen in my tender four years of life.

I would become the clown to be visible to my mother. I would do incredible things like jump off roofs, anything to get my mother's recognition. The neighbors would tell her about my behavior and she didn't appreciate it. It wasn't what I wanted, but it was attention nonetheless.

My father would take me to the movies, the auto races, or to look at cars that he might purchase. He trained me to listen to the sounds of these cars and would test me by asking me what was wrong with each one. Little by little I learned how to diagnose cars by their sounds. My father was my buddy except for those strange looks he would give me that made me feel like he wanted something from me that he could not have. I did not understand. Fear was something I learned to live with. Despite his looks, I felt special because I got the attention I desperately craved.

Chapter 3, The War Years

In August 1941, we moved back across the bay to San Francisco from Mill Valley. Our new home, situated across from Sutro Park, had large cedar and pine trees surrounding it. At night, my imagination wandered as I laid in bed looking out the window at the grand Romanesque and Greek statues that stood as sentries over the gardens. The house was on the corner of 48th Avenue and Geary Street above the Pacific Ocean. Less than a half mile down the street stood the Cliff House, which still remains today. Next door to the Cliff House were the Sutro Baths which had an amusement park inside. There were four bathing pools able to accommodate 250 people; one salt water pool with water from the sea, one hot pool, one cold pool, and a diving pool. I spent most of my time when I was five years old diving off the 20-foot platform. I have always felt I needed to be near water, where I feel safe and at home. An ice skating rink and plenty of slot machines were also part of the Sutro Baths. The huge glass structure enclosing the baths was torn down after the war. What remains today is the Cliff House and Sutro Park; the baths burned in 1966.

There was an amusement park down the street from our house and across from the Pacific Ocean where I would sometimes visit with my cousins. In 1940, the biggest roller coaster on the west coast was situated there. This was a magical time as I had so many places to go and have fun with my cousins even though I was only five. I remember a huge building where unusual mirrors would distort our bodies to all sizes imaginable. A slide that extended from the floor to the ceiling with undulating shapes in the middle made it challenging and fun. The 7-foot tall Laughing Sally whose head moved from side to side, accompanied by a raucous laughter that sometimes frightened me stood outside the Fun House.

I entered kindergarten at Sutro Elementary School on 12th Avenue in September 1941. I was the oldest in the class because my birthday didn't make the cutoff date for when the school year started. I felt strange because not only was I the oldest but I was also the tallest. I did not feel connected to anyone in class.

December 7, on a cold, rainy day, loud sirens exploded during our nap time where we lay on mats in our underwear. In a state of confusion and terror all around me, I jumped up and ran out of the building scared to death. No one stopped me. I ran thirty-six blocks in the pouring rain wearing only my underwear. This may be the beginning of my life of running. When I arrived home, soaked to the bone and frightened, my mother said, "Why did you leave school?"

I said, "When the sirens went off, I was so scared that I had to run home. The teachers were scared too. No one stopped me." We did not know Pearl Harbor had been bombed until the next day. These were terrifying times to live in, everyone walked around in fear believing that today would be their last day alive. President Roosevelt's words, "The only thing to fear is fear itself," were my mother's mantra.

Two weeks later, when I came home from school, I could not believe my eyes. Sutro Park was full of soldiers and tanks. I went over to one of the soldiers and said, "What are you doing in our park?"

He pointed to the Pacific Ocean and said, "We are protecting you from the Japanese." I did not understand.

These wonderful friendly soldiers became my dear friends for a year playing tag, jump rope, and hide and seek. I'm sure I entertained them and gave them a portion of normalcy during a time of uncertainty. To me, they were my playmates. They actually talked to me and asked me questions; I felt acknowledged and visible. I knew they were lonely just like me.

Two of the soldiers would take me down the hill to Sutro Baths. One of the soldiers bet me I could not dive off the platform. I said, "I bet you I can," and I climbed the four flights of stairs to the top of the platform and without any fear dove off and down into the water. The soldiers were shocked that I had done it. My father came to mind as I dove off because for the past few months up until then, my father had challenged me to jump off. He thought, I could not dive off the high platform. I thought to myself, "I'll show you," and dove off the platform feeling like a bird in the air for a split moment.

My mother was pregnant with my brother Tommy. As nightly air raids occurred, we had to all be under tables until the sirens stopped. It was very difficult for my mom who was pregnant and quite large to fit under the table. Dad feared getting drafted. He told us we were going to move to Grass Valley. He would work as a truck driver logging wood, one of the occupations exempt from the draft. I felt very angry having to leave my soldier friends. When I told them we were going to move they became very sad, they told me I had brought pleasure and joy into their lives. We had fun. I felt alive, appreciated, and seen, maybe for the first time in my life.

When I knew my family was going to move, I was about to lose something very special. I would be alone again, without my first friends, isolated and invisible. I felt special and valued when the soldiers gave me a farewell party before we left. It was so unlike the way I felt at home. Leaving them was like leaving a part of myself. They loved me, and in giving that up I gave up a part of me I had never known before.

Chapter 4, Grass Valley

It was to be another adventure according to my father who enthusiastically tried to convince us all, even though we were reluctant to move yet again. "We will have new places to discover, new people to meet, and we will leave the nightly sirens behind."

During Christmas vacation in 1942, we packed the car and headed east towards the foothills of the Sierras. As we crossed over the Bay Bridge, I didn't want to look back because I already missed my soldier friends I had left behind in San Francisco. Dad bribed my sister, brother, and myself with a bonus if we kept silent. He hated to hear us all talk at once. I learned at a young age that silence was rewarded. Our bonus this time would be an ice cream cone waiting for us in Grass Valley if we kept quiet the whole way. Our 1936 Buick was warm and toasty, but soon, a white substance I didn't recognize began hitting the windshield. It was light and cold and it frightened me because I had never seen it before and I thought it was milk. Dad had told us about snow but was this it? Because I had to remain silent, my six year old mind figured this must be "snow." My excitement won over Dad's rule to keep silent. I screamed "Daddy stop!" After a four-hour silent car ride, we all needed to relieve ourselves. Dad pulled over and we all piled out.

My tiny feet sunk into the soft, fluffy white snow. After we turned the snow yellow, we all threw snowballs at each other. The sad feelings about leaving my soldier friends behind finally were lifted. I was thrilled to be playing with my sister and brother and Dad in the snow. And I still got my ice cream cone once we reached Grass Valley.

When we arrived in that beautiful town with snow covered Victorian and Edwardian homes, it felt like a dream until we reached our place. Our home was an ugly, huge, two-story, dark brown, shingled house. It had broken stairs, shingles hanging and dropping off the side. Entering our new home at 122 Blake Street, it looked as though it had been abandoned for years. It was as cold inside, as it was outside. The carpets were old and stained and the wallpaper was torn and dirty. There were many holes filled with paper to keep out the cold, but the paper didn't do a good job. The only source of heat was an ancient gas furnace in what passed for a living room. That furnace's job was to heat the entire two story, three bedroom house. It did a lousy job as the entire family was always cold. We went to bed with layers of clothes on.

Despite its uninviting façade, I loved that house because I found a small room in the attic. I took possession with my paper dolls as wall decorations alongside pictures of cowboys. It was my private hideout. I would go in there and daydream. No one else came up there. It became my first and only room all to myself. I brought blankets and pillows to my special place, in order to sleep there. Sadly, Mom ordered me, "You sleep in your bed next to your sister in your bedroom!" I still went up there for an hour a day, all to myself.

There was big oak tree outside the window where I built a treehouse. I always loved to build places away from the family—I wanted to be alone and let my imagination do what I physically longed to do: run wild.

I had just turned 7 years old there in Grass Valley when I first saw an African American person. She was a child, about 8 years old and looked so scared. This was a time during very strict racial segregation. Black people were not allowed to live with white people. I never had seen anyone so scared before and of course, I could never fully understand her fear, but the fear I sensed from her felt familiar in a way as I knew a similar feeling inside me. She made me aware of this feeling. My secret and fear was that I felt like a boy in a girl's body. After becoming aware of my secret, I played only with boys.

School was a joke. I had the same teacher for three years. How can I ever forget her! She was so outrageous sitting in front of the class every day with her big, heavy legs crossed while she filed her fingernails or painted them sometimes, and she always talked to the class as if we were her friends. She did not feel like our teacher. Sometimes she would read us stories, but most of the time she would talk about her life. She never gave us any instruction. We would work on our own in our workbooks, and I taught myself math and other subjects. My sister used to read stories to me, helping me to learn how to read. I was fascinated with my sister because she was the first person to take the time to teach me something.

My brother George's friends became my buddies because I did not like to play with dolls and do all those things girls did. George had three good friends. One was Will, who had freckles. He would say, "You are fun Ruthie, I wish my sister was like you." Bill, another friend, was short and heavier set and always yelled at me, "I want to be the leader!" There was also Phil, tall and skinny just like my brother. I learned I could lead others as I was elected to be the captain of all the games: kickball, baseball, and soccer. They liked me to be their leader as I was the oldest in the group. We would all go to the movies every Saturday to see Roy Rogers, the Cisco Kid, or the Lone Ranger. We paid 25 cents to enter the film and 5 cents cents for popcorn. Then we would come back to the vacant lot to play cowboys and Indians, riding on broomsticks, pretending they were our horses.

Girls were not allowed to wear pants in 1943—yet another reason for me to want to be a boy. I felt like I was born into the wrong body. I had such penis envy when I watched boys pee standing up. I saved every penny that I earned from collecting bottles and turning them into the grocery store for nickels and dimes. When I finally had saved enough money I bought my first pair of jeans. I was so excited when I put them on that I peed in my brand new jeans. I was devastated but I hid my jeans under stairs at the park where we played cowboys and Indians. There was also enough privacy under the stairs to hide and change my clothes.

Grass Valley was a rich, beautiful town with many flower gardens. I loved to pick flowers from these lovely yards and bring them home to my mother. She loved flowers and she rewarded me with one of her infrequent smiles whenever I came home with one I had picked just for her. When she would say "Thank you," I felt like her hero, I never remember my father giving her anything.

We kids liked to wrap up my baby brother, Tommy, in a blanket and put him down the clothes chute, which went from the second floor of our house to the first floor. Tommy was only one year old at the time. He still remembers it to this day. My baby brother was a real tyrant as he used to break the slats out of his crib or the playpen—he hated to be enclosed in any form. Even today, he told me laughing, "I still remember that!" I find it warmly strange that he still remembers this too.

During this time in Grass Valley I remember putting on a friend's hat. Little did I know it held a colony of lice. A few days later I was scratching my head like mad. My mother put me on her lap to search for the culprits. I was shocked! This was the first time I could remember my mother ever touching me. I froze with fear. I could not process, let alone recognize, this feeling. Our home was emotionally cold and lacked affection. Spankings were the only physical way we were touched. We three kids waited in line outside of the bathroom door, dreading our turn for the spanking. I was my father's favorite so I was never spanked. He would hit the floor with the strap and not my bottom. It felt weird that I was never touched by him but the way he would always stare at me with those lust-filled eyes made me frightened and terribly uncomfortable.

After a year in Grass Valley, my father was injured driving a logging truck and could no longer perform his draft-exempt job. Out of fear of being drafted at 32 into the army, he came home and said, "I am going to Mexico. I don't want to go to war!" My mother went into a panic and became ill from the fear of being left alone with four children. She stayed in bed depressed most of the year. Dottie, my sister, and I took care of my brothers. We had very little money, thank goodness Dad had paid cash for our home. My father fled our home in fear and we were left with no income. My sister and I would go to the corner grocery store and beg for food. We told the Asian store owner about our father's disappearance and he was kind enough to give us bread and cheese for that year my father was gone. Alice, our wonderful neighbor, brought us hot food and loaned my mother money for the utilities. Even though this was a difficult time for us, it was a relief to not have my father and his leering eyes in the house. When I had a toothache, Mother took me to a dentist who accepted credit. The look the dentist gave me was a look I was to see in many old men: a hungry, greedy look. I did not like this man!

It was my first visit with a dentist. His office had red velvet drapes, a red couch, and an old, smelly-mildewed chair. The whole room stank. As my mother waited in the vestibule, I went into his exam room alone, filled with anxiety. I was nervous and didn't know what to expect. As soon as I sat down, he placed a towel around my neck, and his other hand went up my dress! He told me, "Oh, I like you so much!" like if that was supposed to make it okay. I froze in fear, shutting down and trying to not be in my body. My mother liked this old man, so I thought she would not believe me if I told her what he did. I was to have this kind of experience with many dentists in my life. I learned from a young age to be seen and not heard, and to keep silent. I kept my mouth shut and never told her what had happened. Rage grew deep within me that only running and swimming quieted.

When World War II ended, my dad returned home from Mexico. It was wonderful because my mother was so happy. For a year, she had been alone with us children and Alice next door. After Dad returned, we hastily moved back to San Francisco. We owed everyone in town money and Dad couldn't find work. I was very sad to leave my friends once again. That was a pattern of my life, making friends and then leaving them behind because we had to move.

Chapter 5, Daly City 1945–1948

We moved back to the Bay area in the spring of 1945 to a suburb of San Francisco called Daly City. I never liked this area. People were not friendly, no one talked to anyone. Instead of being placed in the fourth grade, I was held back in third grade because I received no education in Grass Valley. I felt humiliated being again older and taller than the other students. I didn't fit in. I would be the oldest in all my classes after that. I don't remember making any friends in school when I was young.

Playing hop scotch, jump rope, and relay races were all I excelled at in those years. Somehow my physical abilities saved me, but not my academics. My sister would read aloud to me, and only that instilled the desire in me to read. I discovered a book called *Amboy Dukes*, reading it under the covers at night with a flashlight, away from the rest of the house. It was my secret, as it was widely stigmatized as pornographic and even banned in Canada. That only made me want to read it more. This was my sexual education and it would tantalize my young, innocent imagination. I looked forward to bedtime in order to finish the novel. It was the first book I ever read.

Our neighbors, who had just arrived from Greece were warm and friendly, such a contrast from my cold and unemotional family. They sent us delicious Greek food—stuffed grape leaves with rice, savory lamb dishes, and baklava. The seasonings were exotic and such a contrast from my family's overcooked vegetables, and dried meat. The vegetables tasted so bad I would put them in my napkin and throw them away when Mom's back was turned. I loved hearing my neighbors speak their language. It was like a song, sounding somehow familiar to my ears.

Hercules, their youngest son, was my buddy. He was an older boy, a whole two years my senior and had the most beautiful brown eyes: warm and inviting. We would play together and I helped him learn English and in exchange he would tell me fascinating stories of his life in Greece. I remember how he described the water, "The Aegean Sea is like a pearl of blue and green, it is so clean you can see your reflection as you look into the water." When I traveled to Greece years later, I was disappointed because I could not see my reflection. The Sea had become so polluted, it turned from green to dark blue.

The summer of 1948 was to usher in a thrilling season. Dad bought a resort in the town of Nice in Lake County. My mother would rent and clean the cabins. Dad would travel the three hours from San Francisco to Nice on the weekends. It had six cabins, each one had a kitchen and a living room.

I loved being back in the country. I could run barefoot and spend my days in the water, where I could return to what felt like the womb and feel safe. The freedom to play and swim all day without a care felt exhilarating. Lake County had many fruit orchards, pears, and apples where people traveled to pick as the harvest neared. I convinced my mother I could make money by picking fruit and doing small jobs for people in the neighborhood. She let me go. I was surprised. The money I gave her was welcomed. Dad never gave her enough and she appreciated my help. During this time, my brother, George and I made many friends. The people who rented our cabins educated us on far away places they had lived.

This began my fascination with people from different countries. Once we had a man from India who stayed for a month. I was mesmerized by him. He would put his small colorful rug down and sit in a yoga position for hours, eating his nuts and raisins. I loved to hear his stories and the music from India he played on his phonograph at night. It stimulated my imagination and stirred the desire in me to go there one day. Fortunately, years later I would have the privilege and good fortune to go.

Lake County becomes very hot in the summer so I would be in the water most of the day. I had my first boyfriend, Carl, that summer in 1948. I was 12 years old and we loved to kiss under the water, as we were both very shy. I never understood why we would never talk to each other when we would get out of the water. Even so, it was a thrilling sensual experience--my first consensual one at that.

Some weekends Dad would take me up in the mountains on the back of his Harley Davidson motorcycle to go deer hunting. To this day Harley Davidsons always get my attention with fond memories of my father. I hated when he killed animals but I was too frightened to say anything to my father. He was a big powerful man. He loved to walk on his huge hands and would continue until the kids would stop clapping. Everything about him was in his hands; they were enormous.

When I was 13, Jeff, a young man who was 18 took me dancing at Cob Mountain. We heard the famous music of Glenn Miller. Jeff was a great dancer so it was so easy to follow his every step. It was a memorable night. I loved dancing and this was the first time I had ever danced with a man. We came home late from the dance. I was so happy with Jeff who danced so well that I forgot about the time and when we arrived at my place my father was in such a rage he almost knocked over the young man's jeep. My father never liked me dating anyone, and he frightened me with his rage so much that I never introduced him to any boyfriend after that experience until I met Joe.

My father had a classic speed boat which I loved to ride in but water skiing was my favorite activity on the immense Clear Lake. This area was not depressed at that time, and the water was not polluted as it is now. Most of the people there are now on welfare.

Another summer spot was where my grandfather, George Archer, built a big beautiful home for all his children and grandchildren before he died, located in Guernewood which is now part of Guerneville. My father had three sisters and two brothers. Sharing the house with our cousins was a significant childhood memory because we rarely saw each other. Christmas was painful because my cousins received expensive presents while my siblings and I did not. The best present I ever got was a softball from my favorite aunt. I felt recognized as she knew I loved sports.

The free amusement park in Guernewood on Highway 12 just off Cazadero Road was the highlight of our evenings. There was a shooting gallery, knock the bottles down, and other games. This gave me the opportunity to hone my physical abilities which I was proud of. The roller skating rink was filled with young people my age. Reconnecting with them each year made me realize how we were getting older. Our bodies were maturing. I would compare my developing breasts with the other girls. Mine were the largest but I felt shamed by their size. It didn't fit with my wanting to be in a boy's body. Denial as usual was my way of coping with feelings.

Nightly movies were shown on a big white screen outside under the stars in the redwoods. My favorites were either Charlie Chaplin, The Marx Brothers, or the Three Stooges and other outrageous comedians. My cousins and I would sit on big redwood logs joyfully eating popcorn. We laughed, cried, and yelled. We never wanted the evening to end.

My mother, being surrounded by in-laws, children, and lots of family noise blossomed into another person. Her loneliness and isolation disappeared. She became filled with joy and the previously unseen smiles became a frequent feature on her face during our time in Guernewood. Some of the best times I remember with my mother were at the river. She loved to stroll the mile long walk among the giant redwoods to the river with us kids as we laughed and joked. Skipping down the road, telling jokes, and singing our favorite song, "Hitler is a jerk, Mussolini is a wienie, Hitler is a jerk, whistle while you work," over and over and over again laughing our heads off. Those two weeks a year with our cousins were memorable as we were only together for these brief periods of time during holidays throughout the year.

As the two weeks ended, the sadness and grief about leaving this idyllic time behind became an unwelcomed reality. All of us felt the same, especially my mother. I would count the days until summer would come once again so I could go back to my two favorite places in the world, Lake County and the Russian River, and days filled with meeting new people, laughter and freedom.

Chapter 6, Generations of Broken Hearts

My grandfather, George Archer, immigrated to America at the beginning of the twentieth century, leaving behind the cold, damp climate of Birmingham, England, an industrial city in the northern part of Europe. He was a master bricklayer and brought his skill to earn money and live in sunny California, specifically San Francisco. He returned to Europe to marry his sweetheart, but she did not want to leave England. He knew many women in Birmingham, and when his sweetheart chose not to leave, he married my grandmother, Margaret. They had grown up together and she always loved him, but the feelings weren't mutual. On the voyage across the Atlantic, my father was born on November 28, 1910, to a cold unaffectionate mother and a preoccupied father, whose life was dedicated to work. This was the beginning of the legacy in my family of people coming together out of necessity and not love.

George Archer, my grandfather was talented and hardworking. He built a dealership where new and used cars were sold, along with a garage and gasoline station all in a triangle in one block. That had never been done before in the world, and it still stands to this day. His home and warehouse were on either side of this huge triangle of a block. All were built out of red brick. Additionally, many of the arch structure buildings in San Francisco, including the huge fireplace in The Palace of Fine Arts were built by my handsome, brilliant grandfather. I adored him even though at first his gentle, affectionate touch was foreign to me. He showed me much kindness. He would pinch my cheek, kiss me, and ask me how I was doing. I never remember anyone else in my family ever kissing me. My family was cold and emotionally shut down, except for Grandpa. The contrast between him and my parents was food to a starving child. Although he died when I was five, I've treasured his memory all my life.

The Great Depression affected my grandfather and all his friends immensely. Although many of his friends committed suicide, George, died of a heart attack at the age 52. Because of his many great accomplishments, his picture was on the front page of the *San Francisco Call Bulletin*, which would later become *The Chronicle*.

My father, Thomas, took after my grandfather, he too was a business genius and was also strong and stubborn. My father's rebellious behavior was demonstrated by his refusal to attend school. My grandparents said my father had to leave home. They valued the free education in America in contrast with Europe's tuition based system. Dad was on his own at 13. He lived with a friend for free, and started to earn money by fixing people's cars. My father was able to assimilate information simply by observation. He watched the mechanics at his father's garage, and taught himself the skills necessary to eventually build cars and sell them. He always had money, but he became frightened of losing it from the effects of the Great Depression. Because of his financial fears, money became an obsession. He used his wits to become self taught in managing the business from both the financial and mechanical aspect. Dad saved his father's business during the Depression by finding people who would help him. No one in his family gave him credit for that. Dad didn't socialize with his siblings. His desperation for affection, which he never received from his parents, made him always try to get kisses from his three sisters. Therefore, the sisters and two brothers did not like him as he was called the black sheep of the family. He wouldn't attend any family gatherings because of this. He would drop us off and leave us with them. They loved my mother and they considered her family. Her father had died and her mother was absent both-- emotionally and physically. My mother was responsible for keeping the entire extended family together.

My father had been a great womanizer all his life. His first love, Isabel, came from a rich San Franciscan family and she was forbidden to marry my father. My father's family was considered working class and beneath them. Dad never got over Isabel. He would confide in me throughout his life and talk about her big legs, which he found very appealing. In fact, he would confide in me about all the women he was involved with. My mother also used me as her confidant, she was in love with an artist, Bruce. He too, was from an affluent family from Carmel. Before her father died he told my mother, "You could not trust an artist. They can never make enough money to support you and a family. Now, Thomas, on the other hand, can make money all the time. You can be sure you'll be well taken care of because there will always be cars to repair."

Dad befriended my mother's father, William, and they would play cards every Friday night. Eventually my father could see how wonderful my mother was with her father, who was crippled from a train running over his legs when he was five years old. He walked elegantly in his artificial legs and my mother took very good care of him. After a year of dating, my parents eloped to Reno in 1932. Dad had his own gas station and fixed cars so they were never poor. My sister Dottie was born in 1934, and I followed in 1936.

My sister was constantly sick with asthma. My mother was sandwiched between taking care of my grandfather and her own growing family. My father and I received very little attention from her. I soon discovered I could get her to notice me if I acted out in school, or jumped off roofs. Then I would have her total attention, even though it was negative. Dad felt my mother's unavailability and began to seek comfort in the arms of other women.

I was uncomfortable being alone with my father. I felt his sexual energy towards me and it terrified me. He never physically touched me, it was all covert. I sensed it but I could never prove it and sometimes I constantly questioned what I was feeling. I would numb my feelings by sneaking into the liquor cabinet in the middle of the night and taking sips of brandy at twelve years old. Between the alcohol and candy I would consume, my teeth suffered to the point of having them all replaced. I was also laying the foundations of my alcoholism. I may have been frightened of his energy but I loved the attention I got from him.

Dad loved to get attention from anybody and everybody. He would show off by walking around the block on his hands. I used to be embarrassed because he would do it so frequently. I would shamefully distance myself from watching his exaggerated need of being on display for everyone to see, even strangers.

After my mother's father died, my father began moving us all over San Francisco. Dad would buy old houses that needed to be rebuilt. After he fixed them he would sell them for a profit, always using his highly honed financial skills. We moved frequently, from the Sunset, to the Richmond, from North Beach, to the Mission. Then there was Miraloma Park, the Excelsior and the Haight Ashbury. I can honestly say I really know San Francisco very well. This taught me to make friends quickly. I would find boys to play sports with and would make new friends immediately.

When Dad bought a resort in Clear Lake, he would come up on Friday nights for the weekends from San Francisco. I loved to ride on the back of his motorcycle. His fancy Harley Davidson was his pride and joy. He had a horrible motorcycle accident one year and was flat on his back in one of the cabins for three months. Those summer months were unusually hot. My mother had to take care of him. She was five months pregnant at the time and miscarried. When I found out what had happened, I felt relief. My mother never complained about anything, she was such a good Catholic. She was emotionally shut down. When we would go to Carmel, she would talk about the love of her life Bruce. She would become animated and happy. She would sit at the dinner table and just smile, as I am sure thoughts of her love affair with Bruce would flood her memory.

Dad's womanizing went on all his life. He went off to Mexico and married three women at different times. Being that Mexico is a Catholic country, traditionally, a woman couldn't sleep with a man unless they were married. He would marry them and then after they became too demanding for him, he would leave them. My father loved to show me photos of them and they looked just like my mother, beautiful, thin, and dark.

The last time my father left for Mexico, my brother George took care of us. Mom came down with a horrible cold and for six months my sister and I took care of her. I think she had a nervous breakdown from all the stress of four children and no family around to help. Each time Dad returned she was so happy to see him. He was her emotional anchor, and each time he left, she became sick, withdrawn, and isolated from us. At twelve years old, I earned money by helping neighbors. I would cut their lawns or help them with errands. I valued one of my father's traits, and that was to be financially independent. I refused to ask my parents for money. When Dad died, he did leave me a very nice inheritance.

When all of us had moved out of our home, my father moved my mother to Yuma, Arizona. He told us, "I can now, finally, have your mom all to myself without any grandchildren running around." This hurt my mother as she loved all of us but it was my father's turn to have all her attention. It was just the two of them until she died in 1999. My father was so afraid of losing money he would not turn on the hot water heater and my mother had to shower in cold water for the last years of her life. He bought cheap food and I could never eat at his home when we would visit them in Yuma.

After Mom's death, my niece Lorraine and my partner Josefina had to drag my father out of Yuma as we knew he would run off and get married to another woman and she would get all the money he had saved and invested. Lorraine brought him to her home and took care of him until he died in 2005.

It has been within the last month that I've begun to have appreciation for my father. I am very much like him. Once I looked into the mirror and saw my father's face looking back at me. I reflect him in his love for being physically active and in being somewhat of a daredevil. Buying old houses and restoring them and loving to travel is another trait I inherited. I witnessed his abusive behavior towards my mother and that prevented me from appreciating him. Since he has died a new awareness has evolved and I can finally have some compassion and appreciation for the old goat that he was.

Chapter 7, Another Broken Heart

Writing about my mother is a challenge due to my conflicting feelings. On one side there is the pure love of a child for a parent and of feeling safe and cared for. On the other side, I never felt my mother loved me, she did the basics, food and clothing, but not love. She declared her appreciation of me only after I graduated from college. She said she was very proud of me. This was the first time I heard her acknowledge me in a positive way, and it shocked me. I was finally seen by my mother; it had never happened before.

My mother demonstrated this coldness toward me by three horrible memories that have been locked inside me for years. First, I called her when I was married and living in Kentucky. She said, "You can't call me it is a long distance call." She hung up and I never heard from her that entire year. She didn't even write me a letter. When I arrived back in San Francisco, I found her lying on her bed. There was no "Hello, glad to see you, I'm happy you're home." What she did say was, "Did you close the front door?" I heard from my sister that my mother began smoking and drinking when I left that year for Louisville, Kentucky.

The third and most painful memory was after my daughter's death. Mom wasn't able to be caring or compassionate. She simply said, "Keep a stiff upper lip." Even though I know that is how she had survived, it did not soothe my pain. Her lack of caring when I was so vulnerable and in desperate need of "mothering" made me realize she couldn't be there for me. In fact, she never had been there for me, and this was the supreme example. This event brought me a realization of my mother's lack of emotional empathy. She didn't have it to give. I took my pain and anger and buried it deep within, and used love addiction to suppress it further. I know she admired how well I could take care of myself. However, I saw the love she had for her sons. No wonder I wanted to be a boy, in my mind they received love simply for being male. When I was young, I didn't care because I knew my father loved me, even though his looks made me uncomfortable.

My mother, Mary, was born in San Francisco in 1912 and told me many stories about my grandmother, Jeanne, whose parents were killed in a fire when she was 15. The family had emigrated to New York from Lyon, France when she was five. There were no other family members living close by so Helen, a close family friend, brought my grandmother Jeanne to San Francisco and raised my grandmother along with her son, William. He loved my grandmother. She was very beautiful, charming and had an exotic foreign manner. Jeanne held onto her French pride acting as if she were somehow better than everyone because of her nationality.

William and Jeanne married when he was 20 and she was 17. A tragedy occurred on their wedding night when he dropped his trousers and Jeanne saw he had artificial legs. My mother told me the story and claimed my grandmother passed out in horror and awoke the next morning extremely ill. Eventually Jeanne had to be hospitalized. When Jeanne found out she was pregnant, she came down with tuberculosis. After my mother was born, Jeanne had to be put in a sanitarium in Los Angeles where the warm heat helped her heal. She stayed in Los Angeles until my mother married my father.

Jeanne was a depressed and needy woman demanding of my mother's full attention. My mother was drained, with very little left for my sister and me. When I was 14, I remember going to Jeanne's-- we called her Nana. I was excited to tell her I was taking French and she said angrily, "I speak French, not you!" Her declaration frightened me and I dropped the class immediately. I did not like her; especially when she would sit and stare at the picture of her dead boyfriend and talk to him. I asked her about this. She would respond dismissively, "You would not understand matters of the heart."

Mom's life was blessed with attention and love from Grandpa William and his mother Helen. Mom went through Catholic school for 14 years as a good student. After graduation, she found employment easily as a secretary. Then she fell in love with Bruce, a rich artist from a well off family in Carmel, California. Grandpa did not like the fact that there was a class distinction between Bruce and my mother Mary. He demanded Mom stop seeing Bruce. She was devastated, but being a good Catholic girl who adored her father, she followed his wishes. Grandpa worked in the city hall as an elevator operator and in his working class status, he felt uncomfortable around Bruce. This occurred during the Depression, and rich people were losing their fortunes. Grandpa feared Mary would marry Bruce who might lose his wealth and then she would be poor. It was for this reason, my grandfather's fear around money, that he never realized how much he had hurt his daughter.

Grandpa met my father, Thomas, one day and invited him to meet my mother. Thomas, or Tom as he was called, was just the kind of man Grandpa liked, a good, hard-working, smart man and with an earning potential. Tom would come to mother's house and play cards with Grandpa every weekend. Mary and Tom were both in love with other people. Tom in love with Isabel, an upper-class woman, and Mary in love with Bruce. They both would talk to me about their other loves. I felt uncomfortable listening to them. *Why were they telling me these stories over and over again?*

My sister, Dottie, was born in 1934, a year after their marriage. She was a sick child. Mom focused her attention and care by attending to Dottie and Grandpa. Grandpa moved in with them after his mother died. Dad received very little of the leftover attention which may explain why he had many affairs. Mom was happy having her father living in her home although my grandfather demanded Mom's constant attention. Soon, Dad started staying out late and not coming home for dinner. When Grandpa died in 1938, Mom's grief turned into depression. It was not until my brother George was born that my mother emerged from her depression. It was two years of gloom and a mother who couldn't parent. Mom exhibited all the signs of postpartum depression, though it was not diagnosed at the time.

Chapter 8, Dottie

My sister, Dorothy Archer, was born on a cold winter night on November 6, 1934, in San Francisco at the height of the Depression. We called her Dottie. Both of her parents wanted a boy and would try again, until my brother was born after me. Dottie was a frail, premature baby who was sick most of her youth. Her asthma and allergies demanded my mother's undivided attention.

Dottie played the piano at a very young age and learned classical music after six months of lessons. She occupied her time with reading because she could not go out and play due to her being a sickly child. She found companionship within the books' characters, which she loved. Mom was always afraid for Dottie's health because she was so fragile and constantly ill.

When Dottie was 14, Mom found Doctor Bear, a specialist for allergies and asthma. When Doctor Bear arrived at our home I was immediately attracted to her. This surprised me, at twelve years old, I had never been attracted to a woman before. She was a tall and handsome Jewish woman with a strong German accent. In the 1936 Olympics in Berlin, Germany, she won a medal for the breast stroke. Hitler was the fuhrer who led the Olympic games in Berlin. The government wanted her to compete because they knew she would win. They planned to send her to the concentration camps after the Olympics. Fortunately, she escaped before the Nazis could find her. She had met James Bear, a doctor visiting from the U.S. and they married.

After examining Dottie, Dr. Bear told her she needed to swim at least three times a week. This began a new life for Dottie. She was a natural in the water. With long legs and arms, she soon made Dr. Bear's water ballet team. Eventually she became a soloist. This 180 degree turn around in her health and her life brought great joy to me. Then her insecurities began to take over. Little did we know that this was the beginning of her mental illness. She began to have panic attacks. There was no medicine at the time for such an illness, but with help from friends she survived.

At 19, she had made friends with a large group of surfers at San Francisco's Ocean Beach. It is called Kelly's cove, which is below the Cliff House. The surf there is treacherous with riptides and currents. It is supposed to be the most difficult place to surf in the world. In the winter months it is almost impossible to enter the water because of the riptides going in and out in every direction. Dottie was the first woman surfer in San Francisco. She would take those huge waves like a shark. Even today the surfers remember her for her skillful body surfing.

At 20, Dottie met John, also a great surfer. They soon married, and Dottie's insecurities made John very uncomfortable as she was always imagining him with other women. They had a daughter together, Lana, but after a few years, they divorced. Dottie won a small settlement and gave the money to me so I could buy a house. The deal was that we would live together, and I would take care of Lana while Dottie went to college. After she started college, Dottie began to drink heavily, staying out all night with different men.

The following year, Dottie met Dick, also a surfer who loved to drink. I went to Reno with them when they got married. Dottie passed out in the back seat from drinking, even though she was pregnant. The marriage was a disaster from the very beginning as Dick felt obligated to marry her. Abortions were unthinkable at that time and very dangerous. Dottie had two daughters with Dick, Lorraine and Karen. Dick suffered from alcoholism and they were always fighting. Now Dottie had genuine reasons to feel frightened. One day she came home and found Dick in bed with her best friend. That did it! She left him, and called me saying she was moving in with a friend of hers, though immediately she took up with another man named Robin, whom she would live with for four years.

Dottie had her first of many nervous breakdowns after that. She had lost custody of her daughters to their fathers. She ran around with hippies from the Haight Ashbury acting crazy. One night she dressed up as a witch and came to my house, knocking at the back window. This scared the hell out of me! She was in and out of mental hospitals. Eventually she was committed to the Napa State Hospital mental ward where she remained for a year. While she was there, she met a man who was visiting. He taught her to chant Nam-Myoho-Renge-Kyo, a Buddhist chant part of the Nichiren Buddhist school.

After several months there was a noticeable change in her demeanor. She stopped hearing voices and began to emerge from her mental illness. She appeared happy and healthy again, and even organized the floor of the ward. It was filthy and ugly, but she made it beautiful. Within two months I was able to take her home with me. Shortly, she began sleeping all the time, from all the pills they gave her. I took her to St Mary's mental ward. She had stopped chanting. She told me, "I am going back to Jesus, he will take care of me." She refused to take responsibility for her own life. It appeared to me she felt content and felt safe in the mental wards. She was cared for, just like Mom used to care for her.

At St. Mary's, Dottie was to meet her third husband, Ken. Ken was very wealthy, handsome, smart, talented, and kind but he too, was mentally ill. Dottie told me Ken's mother molested him. He would ask himself a question and answer it as if he were another person. I was shocked when I met him and heard him talking to himself, but Dottie was happy. That was what was important. A few months after they met, they were both able to go home. They had a big wedding, something Dottie had always wanted. They were content with each other, and Ken eventually began having conversations with other people, and stopped talking to himself. They lived happily together for 17 years, traveling and living the good life Dottie had always wanted.

When Ken died of pneumonia, Dottie soon relapsed into her sick self. She gained a lot of weight, and she was eventually unable to walk. She had a constant bladder infection and had to take antibiotics for ten years. Because of all her illnesses, she needed constant care. At one point, she had gotten stuck in the bathtub for fourteen hours. Her daughters placed her in an assisted living home. There, she was given round the clock care at 72 years old. Three years later, she had another bladder infection. Antibiotics no longer cured it so she remained in the hospital. Karen and Lana and I stayed by her side every day.

Her body was riddled with pain and fever. I saw her daily, but never got a straight answer as to her condition. She was given morphine which did little to stop her moaning. We watched as my sister agonized through a week-long dying process. We felt relief when she passed. I miss my sister although I'm comforted that she is no longer in a body that was continually sick and wracked with pain. My feelings concerning my sister were a mixture of fear of her insanity and love for her when she was not insane. We were close but I never knew what I was going to find when I would visit her. She was the happiest with Ken but at times would become jealous of me. It was definitely a push-pull unstable relationship that I just accepted as part of my life.

Her family and friends remember Dottie not for her illnesses, but for her loving kindness. I cried all day at her funeral, because she was my only sister. I miss her. Even though she was always sick, she was a love and we were close. She was my first friend and I knew she cared for me even though we had our moments of big disagreements.

In 2016, my sister was in a documentary about women surfers in San Francisco. The winter surf in San Francisco is the toughest in the world and my sister was the first woman surfer there so naturally she played a major role in this documentary. It makes me happy she was recognized, she lived such a painful life. What is interesting is that her second daughter, Lorraine, who was extremely uncomfortable with her mother's emotional condition, basically played a major role in the making of the documentary.

Chapter 9, The Titanium Man

On a bright sunny morning in Mill Valley, my sister and I were playing with my father on the living room floor. I turned my head as I heard the front door open, and my eyes landed on my mother's brilliant smile. It looked out of place, something I had never remembered seeing. I felt like my mother was another person, I had never seen her so happy. She had just arrived home from the hospital in a taxi, and in her arms she carried my baby brother, George. She proudly showed each of us her treasure. When I got to see him, I saw his tiny face twisted with fear in his soft white blanket.

My father's jealousy of George became a big problem in our home. Dad resented all the attention my mother showered upon her only son. Dad complained and yelled like an unloved child. His anger became a painful austerity for the entire family.

My sister Dottie would dress George in our dresses and they played together with her dolls. He loved it. Dad would call George a sissy. My brother longed for my father's appreciation. Dad would catch George in dresses, and would name call and degrade George throughout his life. When George was five years old, he accidentally hit himself in the back of his head with an ax. He hid this fact from the family and wouldn't take off his hat for days. Finally, my mother got him to take off his hat, and discovered a huge blood clot on the back of his head. George said, "See mommy? I am not a sissy." I'm sure he hoped Dad would realize that also.

When George was seven, my father took my sister and two of our friends, on a fishing trip in Clear Lake, California. It was a scorching hot day. All of us except George jumped off the boat and into the water to cool ourselves off from the heat. I looked at George. He was frozen with fear. His face was twisted with anguish, tears flowing down his face. Dad shouted, "Stop being a sissy!" When we returned home, George screamed to Mom, "I not goin' fitten with my daddy no more." My father's emotional abuse continued throughout George's youth until he was thirteen when my father went to Mexico for the third time.

The summer of 1953, Dad left us without any money to survive, again. George was thirteen at that time, and caddying at the local golf course. His income as a caddy went to support us. He was a such a natural athlete that he became a great golfer. Obstacles immediately appeared to aggravate this hopeful turn of events. He was 6 feet 2 inches at such a young age. A doctor told my mother that he should not play golf because of his height. The doctor stated, it would eventually wear down the joints in his body.

George ignored the doctor's advice as he was winning big money against other golfers, betting that he could make certain long distance shots or short putts. He always had hundred-dollar bills in his money belt, and he supported us for 6 months during my father's time in Mexico. When George entered amateur tournaments, he would either win or place in the top three. He was a natural champion.

George's biggest problem was a learning disability, which I believe came from all my father's abuse. Throughout his school years he copied other people's tests to pass exams, yet in his senior year at San Mateo High School, he was offered a scholarship to Santa Clara University for his golfing. He naturally refused for fear of his disability becoming known, and he became an amateur golfer.

Once he was in a tournament in Palm Springs and my other brother Tom and I went with him. We could only find a motel with a double bed so George put a golf club down the center of the bed and told me, "You sleep on that side of the bed and I will sleep on this side." He was such a proper young man with very strong boundaries.

In 1960, George was to meet Mr. Scavenger, the owner of a big beer company called Lucky Lager. To become a professional golfer, George needed a sponsor, and Mr. Scavenger wanted the job. He also gave something to my brother that he never received from our father: appreciation and respect. Mr. Scavenger loved George. At the age of 24, George became a professional golfer. He was now 6 feet and 6 inches tall.

George met the love of his life, Donna, who would shelter him from the public knowing he could not read. George's career soared, but his insecurity about not being able to read frightened him so much that he created a wonderful front as a charmer. He never learned to read, even though my mother would spend hours trying to help him. He went on to win many big professional tournaments in the U.S. and in Europe. The 1969 Masters and the 1971 U.S. Open were his biggest victories.

Sadly, I would only see George on television. By this time, he had totally rejected me for being a lesbian. He didn't want to be associated with anything abnormal because I think he felt so abnormal himself. Although his life was rich with friends and success, my mother would tell me that his fear of people's discovering his disability haunted him. Because of such a busy schedule, he never sought professional help, so he remained frozen with fear. Fortunately, his loving wife Donna was always at his side.

After years of being a famous golfer, at the age of 62, George was diagnosed with cancer. He refused to see me still, harboring feelings about my lesbianism. The rest of my family watched his body shrink almost to a skeleton before he died. I was not a witness, and only knew of his failing through telephone calls from Donna.

By the end of his life, George's greatest victory was clear: he was well loved. At his funeral, there were 15 Golf Champions in their green jackets, winners of the Master Golf tournament. He never forgave our father. However, George had shown him he was not a sissy. Interestingly enough, my father died only six months before George. George refused to attend Dad's funeral. George may have rejected me, yet I knew he loved me. I never stopped loving him and feel such pride as I think about all he overcame. As I wrote these words, I cried for the first time about our loss of closeness. My pride is overwhelming as I recently discovered that George has been inducted into the Sports Hall of Fame! In 2015, a life size photo of George at the San Francisco Harding Golf Course was installed along with his golf bag and shoes. He is one of San Francisco's famous golfers. My brother certainly proved he was not a sissy! Even with all the abuse he received from my father.

Chapter 10, Tommy

August 1944 was a horrible time. World War II, a thunderous bloody adventure across the Pacific, was causing people great anxiety. I remember my parents taking my sister Dottie and me to Mr. and Mrs. Lightford's farm in Lake County for the month. I was eight years old. My parents paid the Lightfords' for our care. I do not remember my parents saying goodbye when they left. They just dropped us off like a package, so typical of their unavailability. My mother was very pregnant with my youngest brother, Tommy. He was born on August 18, 1944. Leaving us with the Lightfords gave Mom time for delivery and recovery. But she never really recovered.

Mr. Lightford was warm, and I liked him and the attention he gave us, until one day he took me for a walk and dropped his pants exposing himself. I ran back to the house and begged Dottie to run away with me but she said no. To have to stay in that house with a creepy man frightened the hell out of me. That same night a black cat jumped from the window above my head and landed on my face. I have always hated black cats ever since that incident.

Mom spent most of her days in bed as she was too frightened to face her life. Tommy was an angry little boy, he was always yelling because he was not getting the attention he needed, something I could relate to since I didn't get it either. George, was Mom's favorite. He got all her attention and Tommy knew it.

Tommy expressed his rage by breaking the slates of his playpen, throwing food against the wall, and screaming. Tommy did not learn how to read until he was married, so school for him became a constant punishment. He did become a loving little boy and learned how to get attention from all the women in the neighborhood. He made many friends, and their mothers adored him. They gave him some of the nurturing he had lacked at home.

When the war ended, Dad came home from Mexico in December 1945. Tommy craved his attention and would do anything to receive it. He always worked for Dad no matter what kind of jobs my father would give him. He worked on cars, constructed buildings, and made deliveries for Dad's furniture store. Dad constantly belittled Tommy, but he took it without complaining.

Mom was too busy protecting George from Dad's abusive behavior to have time for Tommy. Fortunately, Dad was gone a lot of the time. Since my mother did not have any real love for Dad, he was off chasing other women. We were always happy when he was away because there would then be peace in the house.

Tommy was also terribly accident prone. Maybe this was another way he learned to get attention as he still has the same problem to this day. He has had so many concussions it is surprising he is still alive. He was always getting into horrible accidents on his bike or the dune buggies he built. When he lived with me as an adult, he almost burned my house down when he was cleaning the garage with gasoline to get the car grease off the cement and it caught fire.

In 1961, at 16, Tommy got his driver's license and became obsessed with cars, building them and fixing them. For all his accident prone tendencies, he never got into a car accident. That same year, Tommy quit high school and worked for Dad. At age 17, in 1964, he joined the Navy during the Vietnam War; he didn't want to get drafted into the army. He hated war, so he managed to go AWOL every time his ship was going to Vietnam. Sometimes he ended up in the brig. Other times, he was put into the hospital for mental problems. He cleverly managed to stay out of the horrors of war even though he was in the Navy for four years.

Tommy married Dottie's neighbor, Jamie, after he got out of the Navy in 1968. They met when he was on leave one weekend and it was love at first sight. They got married right after his discharge. To support himself and Jamie, Tommy began working as a mechanic right away as he loved cars as much as ever. They lived in San Francisco for three years. After Irene, their only child, was born, they moved to Guerneville.

It was a good move. They had found a gorgeous lot on top of a mountain with a view overlooking an entire forest of trees. It is breathtaking to be there, and sparked Tommy's and Jamie's creative spirits. They built a beautiful geodesic dome with extensions off of it with various shaped colors of glass and different kinds of wood to make it even more interesting. It is a work of art and has appeared in many magazines.

I remember when the dome was just in the embryonic stages. They were living in a tent when I happened to find a book about surviving in the wilderness. It said, "Do not put a tent under a tree with many branches." What did we city folks know? Thank goodness I told them as we had a terrible stormy winter in 1971. Many branches fell off the tree where they had originally placed their tent. If it still stood, it would've crushed them.

Tommy is a great builder and has created a gorgeous environment which people love to visit. He is a generous, loving man who can never say no to anyone. Everyone in our family just adores him, and we are so grateful and blessed to have him alive. He has had two heart attacks in one month. The last heart attack happened in late July 2012. He was alone, hiking in the mountains. Another hiker happened by and discovered him. He was airlifted to the hospital. It was truly a miracle that he was found. Because of his heart of gold, my fearless brother cannot be defeated and has turned survival into his mission. It is a miracle he is still with us.

I find it quite interesting that both of my brothers married women who are Capricorns like me and my sister Dottie married a man who was Capricorn. I think they all liked our strength and our ability to handle money; we never give up. After all, my father's god was money.

Chapter 11, The Citadel of Conformity

My mother felt going to the new Catholic school in our neighborhood would provide us with a better education than the city schools. St. Brendan's is located on Portola Drive below Mt. Davidson between St. Francis Wood and Forest Hill, which are both very affluent neighborhoods in San Francisco. We lived in the poor area where mostly working-class people lived. I started at St. Brendan's in the 6th grade. On my first day of school, I knew I was from a different social class from all the other students even though we all had to wear uniforms. The girls carried themselves with such confidence I had never seen before. We wore gray wool skirts and vests with white blouses and a wine-colored ribbon around the collar of our blouses. Boys wore black corduroy pants and white shirts. We were all well-behaved or gave that appearance.

The Dominican nuns at this school wore long white habits with black rosaries hanging down their sides. They stood solemnly with their white gowns and black veils over their heads and down their backs with a white wimple around their faces. These nuns were brought out to California from the East Coast. They were supposed to be the best educators.

I was a part of the first graduating class, which made our 6th grade the highest in the new school. Sister Alice Joseph would say regularly that we must set an example for the other students. I was there for three years as each year a higher grade was added. Every day we had to line up in single file, entering the classroom quietly from the schoolyard. It felt like a military school. When Sister walked into the room in the morning, we stood up like soldiers and would say, "Good morning, Sister," in unison; and she would reply, sternly, "Good morning. Be seated."

I was the wild one and knew I did not belong, but I had to go to school. Once my father had to come to school because of my poor behavior, and Sister Alice Joseph spoke to him right in front of me. She said, "I don't know what I'm going to do with your daughter, Mr. Archer. She's always talking in line or in class." My father was dressed in his dirty working clothes, he had no shame. I felt shame because all the other students' parents were dressed up when they came to our school.

My father said confidently "Why don't you make her stay after school?" He knew that was my favorite time of day when I would go home and play football with the other boys in the neighborhood. But the after-school punishment began a fascinating discovery time for me to find out what was under those nuns' big habits.

I was given the job of cleaning the windows in the building where the nuns lived across from the school. One day I climbed up on the roofs to peek through the skylight. I was shocked when I saw the nuns! They had short cropped hair and were laughing and carrying on just like us kids. I immediately thought that I wanted to become a nun. They were having such a good time! I loved my new punishment, and I was glad every time Sister Alice Joseph would catch me doing something I should not be doing.

Jerry Brown, our present California Governor, and I were in the same grade. When I played kickball or other sports with my friends, I would notice Jerry walking around the courtyard alone, with a concentrated look on his face. I would talk to him in line going into class — the girls and boys would be separated in two lines side-by-side, so he would be right next to me. I can't recall what we talked about, but we became friends nevertheless. We would whisper to each other in class, and many times I would copy his tests. Our chattiness was often noticed by the Sister Alice, who would make us stay after school. No other students ever had to stay after school besides Jerry and I. We were the two misfits.

To be honest: religion bored me. Every time I asked a question, nobody would answer. I was told to pray about it. Jesus dying on the cross and other stories they told us did not make sense to me. The guilt and fear, the Ten Commandments, the Virgin Mary—I could never wrap my head around these stories.

I felt academically inadequate in the classroom as I had had such a poor education. The only way I got through the day was to copy from Jerry, or whoever was next to me. I remember religion was brought into all the subjects except math. I liked math and felt some success, but not much. I could never figure out word problems. One of the only times I felt adequate and recognized was when in 7th grade, I won first prize in the Halloween parade for a costume I made out of a large, old bird cage. I cut out the bottom, painted it gold, and on a piece of cardboard attached with wire, I had written, "I am a bird in a gilded cage." Everyone else wore costumes they had bought, but I had to be creative. My parents *never* gave me money.

Beyond academics, I enjoyed acting and singing. We put on school plays, and I had the lead in two of them, first as the founder of the girl scouts and then as Joan of Arc. They said I was good, but I must have performed in a blacked-out state, as I could not recall anything about it. I would sing in the chorus every Sunday at the 8 a.m. mass. I loved singing, especially 'Ave Maria'.

One time I remember hearing my voice speak out forcefully. Sister Alice Joseph had blamed another student for something he did not do. I was scared to say anything, but I remember standing and speaking up loudly, "It's not fair! Tommy was not the one talking!" I was punished, but, as I have said, I loved my punishment! I felt strong and powerful that I actually could open my mouth and speak out.

By the 7th grade, I had developed large breasts which made it very difficult to run. I decided that I had to create something to stop them from bouncing, which was very uncomfortable. I made bust-binders out of rags tied around my breasts. This was a perfect solution. I looked flat-chested—just what I wanted. Unfortunately, there was a day while playing football that I was tackled at the legs and fell forward on my breasts. The pain was overpowering. I wanted to continue to play, to be one of the boys, but I had to admit to myself I was a girl. Even though I would still play so many other sports, football was the most exciting — my big love. I would mow lawns and do anything to make enough money to go with my brother George to watch the 49ers football team play at Kezar Stadium. So to have to give up playing tackle football—I felt discarded.

The next challenge of my adolescence occurred one day when I stood up and saw there was blood all over my seat. I was so embarrassed, I jumped up and ran a whole mile home, terrified. No one had ever told me about girls having monthly periods. When I got home, my mother gave me a Kotex pad, said "put it on," and nothing else. I found out from other girls what had happened to me.

The world of sports was my escape and my only reward in those three years at St. Brendan's. It was the only subject at which I excelled, and I was always the captain of the teams. I knew how to organize the girls in kickball, softball and volleyball, and I was so good that the boys would let me play with them in basketball. In 7th grade, I ran in competitions held by the city's Park and Recreations Department, and was the second fastest runner in San Francisco. Because of my recognition, one of the priests of the school, Father Pritchard and I began the first Catholic girls' grammar school sports league in San Francisco. We all wanted to be able to compete with other schools.

Father Pritchard was a young priest who was responsible for helping the teachers and the students. He and I were very close given that he was so involved with the sports leagues. I loved him: he was a very handsome, kind, and loving human being. He would express his appreciation for us, his team, all of the time. Close to the end of that school year, on a sunny Friday, I went to confession. I told him something that was hurting me: my best friend's boyfriend had kissed me. After confession, he walked out of the church alongside me, silently staring at me. I looked up into his eyes and saw *the look*. I knew *that look*! It was not the friendly look I was used to, it was desire. It was the same look I saw in my father's eyes. I had never sensed it before from Father Pritchard. I could no longer feel comfortable being with him after that. There was no running away from him, from that discomfort. Any thought process of escape was out of the question. I needed him and felt trapped. He brought recognition to my life as an athlete and a leader. For our basketball, softball, and volleyball teams, he was the coach and I was elected team captain. We would communicate about the games and how to help the players, but from that moment on, I was frightened. I could never look into his eyes again. I had lost my friend, though I didn't know it at the time. I felt betrayed. I had become used to the feeling, because I needed my father, too. I loved them both, but it was a painful kind of love. I loved these men but I felt no safety with them.

I think I always felt caged in at St. Brendan's. The school day started at 8:30 a.m. with an hour for lunch at noon, then the day ended at 3:30 p.m. We sat in rows, prohibited from leaving our seats for hours. I had no attention span for the lessons and learning. Though I could read, I could not understand concepts. Nothing made sense to me as it did for everyone else around me, those fortunate to have had a quality elementary education. While the others learned, I would watch the clock, with fear and anxiety leaving me jittery for recess, lunch time, or the end of the school day. Moving was the only release I had—my athletic ability was all I could depend on.

Twenty years later, in 1970 at the class reunion, I heard that Sister Alice Joseph used to talk about me with fond memories of my creativity. I also re-encountered Jerry Brown there, who had just recently been elected California's Secretary of State. At the 60th reunion in 2010, I was to learn that Father Pritchard had been removed from the Priesthood for molesting children.

Fear was my motivation. That is why I could never learn in school. I inherited a strength from my father, that came out in my athletic ability. But fear kept me running.

Chapter 12, 1950: Having Fun Discovering San Francisco

When I was 14, we moved once again. This time my father bought an old apartment building in the Haight-Ashbury on Webster Street. He had renovated one of the apartments on the third floor and we moved into it. I was excited and fascinated with this move. It was no longer one of our usual white, poor, or middle class neighborhoods. We did not live in the shadow of poverty. My father always made me and my siblings feel we were poor as he would never give us any money. My mother instilled in us the work ethic of working for our own money. She had one outfit for special occasions that she wore every Sunday, or when we would visit relatives. Money was the "big issue" in the household and the source of many arguments. My mother, a product of her generation where women stayed at home and were taken care of, did not understand my father's tight-fistedness with money. My father had witnessed suicides of his father's friends during the crash of 1929. It was the effect of the financial depression that resulted in his fear of not having money.

This move to the Haight Ashbury occurred during my last six months at St Brendan's. While we lived on Webster Street, I could not tell anyone where I was living. St Brendan's was a popular school, with many applicants. If they'd known I lived out of their district, I would have had to transfer schools. I took two buses daily across the city to get to school, and I loved it. I had another secret life: I was an out of district transfer.

The family on the first floor of our building was from Iran. The wife cooked with an exotic seasoning that I shall never forget, but that I never discovered the name of. I would sit on the hallway stairs, letting this spicy scent, combined with the sounds of foreign drums and stringed instruments, put me into a hypnotic trance. Outside it would be raining, and the combination of smells, music, and the constant drumming of the rain on the building, took me to another world. This triggered the memory of the Indian man I saw doing yoga up in Lake County several years previous, stimulating my imagination to know these countries. I loved to hear music not familiar to my ears, to hear the singing and speaking in a language I did not understand. Once again my fascination with a foreign culture was stimulated.

The Fillmore District at that time was full of black people; I loved it. They were filled with life and their brilliant-colored clothes stood out like rainbows. Women and men dressed in shirts and dresses that were yellow, red, orange or purple. Big straw or felt hats with large feathers stood out as if they were in a daily Easter parade. Men wore striped Zoot suits with gold chains hanging down the sides of their pants. They would swing them in a circle as they strutted down the street to the loud jazz music blasting from the many clubs that lined Fillmore Street. Gospel choirs could be heard singing in the morning from basements of churches. Then the people flowed out onto the streets, socializing, laughing, and having the time of their lives. I was told by my mother not to go down to that area, so I could never tell her how safe and fun it was. It a secret that I treasured.

My father had also bought an ice cream parlor on the corner of 18th and Dolores Street in the heart of the Mission District. I worked every Saturday morning in the parlor making ice cream cones for the diverse crowd who frequented the parlor. I also ate so much ice cream I broke out with a face full of pimples. That made me cut back on the ice cream in a hurry!

The Mission District was full of Latinos, and I loved their music, the people speaking Spanish, and all the smells of Latino food. I started to dress as a pachuco, which is a young and tough Mexican American male. I slicked my hair back with Vaseline into The D/A or duck's ass. This was the height of the male hair style of the day which Elvis Presley sported. I bought black jeans, bright yellow and fuchsia satin jackets, and tan moccasins with black-tire soles. When I walked down Mission Street listening to the loud Latino music, wearing the clothes that I could only wear there, something inside of me reveled in joy. There was power in taking on the male persona as I walked down the street. I was able to finally express that hidden male part of me.

These male clothes needed to be hidden from my family. Before I would go into my home, I would sneak down to the basement of our building. The basement was my secret hideout. I would decorate the tiny area with old bed sheets for privacy, wishing it would keep everyone away. I would change into my "girl clothes" in public restrooms fearing that I would be caught any where close to home. Inside my refuge I would hide my secret life behind stacks of old suitcases, out of sight from prying eyes.

Inside this area I would smoke cigarettes purchased for 5 cents each from the corner store. I would listen to rock and roll like Elvis but loved the black singers and that strong bass beat that matched the beating of my heart. I loved the "high" I would get with each puff of smoke. One day my father asked me to help him move someone. I sat in the back of the truck on a soft comfortable couch, wearing my jeans and smoking my cigarettes. I was hidden from my father's sight. Smoking out in the open air, made me feel tough and strong.

The bust binders I wore began to hurt my chest. I stopped wearing them. As soon as my big breasts were freed from their entrapment, all the boys wanted to take me to the movies so they could try to feel me up. These were my old buddies whom I played sports with, I was one of the boys. Then came these growing breasts that changed my relationship with them. I went out with them hoping the next date would be different. It never was. They were so awkward and clumsy as if following a script told to them by the first one, and then the second, and so on. I asked one of the boys, "Why do all of you just think you can touch me like that?"

He said, "We have had bets on who was going to score with you." After that, I never went out with any of those boys again. But I was conflicted. I enjoyed the closeness but not their paws on my breasts. When graduation came, I was glad to leave that school where I felt all the boys had betrayed me. I thought they were my friends; but in the long run, their teenage hormones got the best of them.

Every day was a new adventure during the six months we lived in that apartment house. One memory, which stands out in my mind, is of a woman running out of her house in a long tight nightgown crying out for her man not to leave her. I had never seen such emotions out in the open before; I thought that happened only in the movies. There were such interesting people on the buses, like an old woman who was blind, but was able to find her way around, or people talking to each other in a friendly manner, which was not common in the other areas of San Francisco.

My mother hated living in the Haight-Ashbury. She missed having a garden and because she didn't make friends she was lonely. My sister told her that I was going down to the Fillmore on Sundays to watch the "Easter Parade" of colorful black people leaving their churches. Her anger spilled over to my father and influenced his decision to move yet again. The day after I graduated from grammar school, we moved to the Sunset District. Its population was primarily white middle-class people; how boring that was!

Little did I know my early life moving throughout the city stimulated a strong desire to travel around the world. Perhaps it was to recapture my youth and integrate all those various cultures I grew up around that I felt had become aspects of myself.

Chapter 13, The Magical Summer of 1950

In the summer of 1950, my sister, Dottie, had to have all her teeth removed because of a severe gum disease. There were no antibiotics at that time. Her gums needed to heal before she could have her false teeth put in. She was fifteen and toothless. This was embarrassing for me but it never seemed to bother Dottie. She would hide it so well by using long scarves that she wrapped around her mouth and neck as if holding a magical wand, waving their ends in front of her to distract people's attention. She had lively conversations with people, and no one ever guessed she didn't have teeth in her mouth. She became more outgoing; I was amazed at her self confidence. Later I realized her confidence increased because she was no longer in pain.

My father bought a house trailer so we could stay in Blue Lake's Le Trianon Resort for the summer while Dottie healed. It is a very special place and the lake is so small you can swim from one side to the other. It has beautiful, big trees with huge branches jutting out over the water. Standing on the branches, we would swing out into the lake on ropes, and fall into the water. Sometimes we liked to dive off the branches, which was thrilling as they bent down and dove with us into the water.

The resort had a huge open-air dance hall. The big, hardwood floor was a meeting place for many young people. Dottie was the most popular girl on the dance floor, with most of the boys flocking to dance with her. We would dance late every night until Mom would have to drag us home.

After a week of fun at the lake and dance hall, I saw a young man doing a perfect swan dive off the diving board at the lake. I was immediately drawn to him. He looked like Tarzan with his big, handsome body, tanned from being in the sun, curly brown hair, and hazel eyes that took me to places I had never been before. I walked up to him, "Oh, you're such a great diver! What's your name?"

"Stan," he said, then he said to me, "You're a good diver, too."

That did it. I fell in love with him instantly and felt like he was an old friend. We became inseparable — swimming and diving, hiking in the hills, horseback riding, sailing. We did everything together. He was so charming, warm, and loving, I just adored him. However, we had a couple of big problems: he had been drafted into the army, and was to report to Fort Ord down in the Central Valley on

September 1st. He was nervous about going off to the Korean war. The other problem was that my mother did not like him. She would say he was too old for me as I was only 14 and he was 18. I never understood what she meant, and I did not care. I was too much in love to listen to my mother.

Because Stan was a man and not a kid, he was aware of the laws and would never make love to me. I would beg him and all he would say is, "You are too young." I was obsessed with wanting to see his penis as I had never seen one before. I knew he had a big one as I could see the bulge in his bathing suit. I became so obsessed I found a place behind the male dressing-room near the lake in the back where no one could see me. I carved a hole so I could peek in as long as I wanted to stare at these men with their penises hanging down their legs. I was shocked as they looked so ugly to me. I never got to see Stan's penis so I would imagine it was as good looking as he was. I never told anyone about my spying; it was another one of my secrets.

When the summer came to an end, Stan became depressed. He was going to go to war in Korea, which seemed like another planet. He said he did not want to go. He was not a man of war. He was a lover of life and hated violence. The last week before he was to leave, he became very sad and withdrawn. It felt like the Stan I loved had already left. He did not even say good-bye to me because he was so depressed.

Chapter 14, High School & The Lost Virgin

For me, high school was just one big fiasco as I never fit in with the other classmates. Everybody had a clique and I was an outsider because of how shy I was. I felt uncomfortable in my skin especially because of my huge breasts. I became dependent on food to fill in the gap left from Stan—he never wrote to me. I had gained so much weight that only an overcoat would somewhat hide my belly and huge breasts. It was uncomfortable for me to go to school every day. My mother had enrolled me in Saint Rose Academy for Girls, but I did not want to go to Catholic school any longer. After I cut class for three weeks, Mom permitted me to go to a public school. I chose Polytechnic High School because they had the best sports teams. I was interested in observing champion athletes. There were no sports for girls at that time in the high schools so the closest I could get to the sports was to watch from the bleachers. Still, it was a turning point in my life. I exploded with joy as I climbed up the stairs of Poly High.

I edged into my first class timidly. Never had I seen so many people in a school before. It felt like a thousand students were dashing to their classes all at once. I was so shy as I knew no one, but the excitement of the school's sports culture was gravitating. I could not wait to get home where I could process the emotions that I had that first day of high school.

We now lived in the Sunset District, and I would take the bus to school every day reading the green sports page in the San Francisco Chronicle. I became a scholar of sports. It was my passion along with being a spectator of sports. I loved to take my brother George to the 49er football games at Kezar Stadium across the street from Polytechnic High School on weekends.

My best class was physical education with my favorite teacher, Mrs. Alvarado. She always taught us with a spirit of joy. It was so much fun to go to her class every day. She was my mentor— an absolute love who tried to give each of us individualized help. I raced to her class every day even though I hated how fat I felt in the dark blue gym suits we were required to wear.

Polytechnic High School was a trade school. I wanted to take the boys' classes, especially auto mechanics, woodshop, and metal shop. These were the classes that interested me. Of course, in 1950, I was not permitted to take these classes, because I was a girl. I had to take sewing, cooking, and typing, which I did not like. Academic classes did not interest me either.

I went to all the games: football, basketball, baseball, and even the unpopular track meets. Poly had the best athletes and I would watch them with such jealousy, wanting to be a boy. They had the power, strength, and recognition; I was envious. High school was such a drastic change from grammar school for me—I went from being the leader of all the athletic teams to suddenly being told that since I was a girl, I was not allowed to play sports. It was extremely frustrating to go from being an athlete to an observer. I hated being a female and this further fueled my desire to be a male.

I also missed Stan so much that I would become depressed if I didn't keep myself busy. I made one friend during this time, Maria. She too missed her boyfriend who was at sea in the Navy. We would talk everyday about our boyfriends and how much we missed them. At least her boyfriend wrote to her. I never received any letters from Stan, only a gold bracelet that had his name on one side and mine on the other. Maybe he could not write, I thought.

Ice cream, french fries, and soda was all my diet consisted of. At dinner I would put my vegetables in a napkin and drop them in the garbage can. I hated vegetables, however, my mouth felt polluted from all the sugar I would eat.

Pictures of my favorite athletes were all over my bedroom walls as I would dream of becoming one of them. I read only books on sports and movies, as they too became my passion and escape. My real life had become too painful as Mom sent me to another abusive dentist, Dr. Orwitz. He would be the last dentist to put his hand up my dress. I couldn't stop him because I blacked-out and chose not to remember what he had done, but carried the deep shame with me. After the visits to the dentist I would flee to the movies to escape the indescribable feelings I had every time I was forced to go to that horrible man.

It was during this same time period that Dr. Bear had come into our lives to help Dottie with her asthma attacks, leading her to join Dr. Bear's water ballet team. I was so attracted to Dr. Bear that I fought to prove myself a great swimmer to be around her even more, which in the end got me onto the team as well. After six months of training, I lost 15 pounds and Dottie's health improved tremendously. Dottie and I finally became friends as we now had something in common.

In October of my second year of high school, I saw Joe coming out of the main building. I felt a strong connection to him—he felt very familiar as if part of me already knew him. I wouldn't fall in love with him, but was strongly attracted to his gorgeous body. He had a broad, muscular back and an excellent build. He didn't talk to me, however, and when I would ask him what he felt or thought, his answer was always the same, "Nothing."

Joe was so popular and friendly with everyone, but with me he was shut down. He could only talk about sports. His dazzling smile made it possible for him to be voted the most handsome and popular senior at Poly High in 1952.

I was only a sophomore but I was infatuated with him. He helped fill the emptiness left by Stan's absence; he was my rebound. Joe saved my life from loneliness and overeating after Stan left. Joe and I began to go to movies, dances, and school sporting events. We became boyfriend and girlfriend.

When Joe bought his first car, a 1940 Hudson, our relationship became more physical. We had our own self-enclosed living room, complete with a couch and wheels! One day he took me up to Twin Peaks and said he wanted to show me something. After he parked the car he pulled out his huge penis and smiled, that dazzling smile. I was shocked. It made me sick and frightened at the same time because I had never seen one so huge. I said, "I want to go home."

As he zippered up he told me, "The other guys in school are jealous of my big penis." I don't know why, but after hearing him tell me that, I began to have fantasies about his penis and wondered how it would feel inside of me.

I felt so special because he was the most popular boy in the senior class and he had chosen me. I was curious to discover what this sex-thing was all about. He always wanted to have sex with me because every time he would be close to me his penis would bulge, straining against his pants. It reverberated the unspoken words of my father as Dad observed me maturing into a woman's body. My father said to me, "You'll only be good for sex," and would repeat this over and over again to me. I believed him and viewed this as my value.

Five months after we met, Joe and I went to a motel. It was his idea and he paid for it. This would be my first consensual sexual experience, and the tingling arousal feelings, mixed with excitement and fear made me want to explore this part of my life. Joe and I took off our clothes and jumped into bed. There was no verbal or physical foreplay and we were both petrified. He gently entered me and within a few minutes, he came. It was over as quickly as it began. We fucked. I just laid there, not feeling anything, not being present in my body. When I returned to my body and saw the blood stained sheets, I panicked. I was raised to believe that if you had sex with someone, you married them. I did not love Joe and didn't want to get married. Yet unconsciously I knew that he would be my future husband. We left the motel within an hour. Sex with Joe became a routine at the drive-in movies on Friday nights. I loved his body, his skin, and I loved to touch him. Being with him brought me pleasure, however, I never reached an orgasm. That wouldn't happen until I was 35 years old.

Joe's family became my family. They were from Greece, warm, loving, and they adored me. I craved this attention as I never received it from my own family. The memory of Stan slowly began to disappear. After a year of going steady, Joe and I went to my house one day. There in the kitchen with my mother, stood Stan holding a bottle of brandy, drunk. He smiled at me. My heart dropped to the floor. All the love I had for him came rushing back, and I wanted to run off with him. However, my commitment to Joe kept me frozen and silent. I stuffed my feelings following my mother's lead, because she knew best, or so I thought. Stan left with tears in his eyes, and I never saw him again.

Joe did not even ask about Stan, and to my surprise, my mother said, "Joe is better for you." She had a warm, motherly relationship towards Joe. He reciprocated in kind because his mother, Despina, had been beaten to death by the mob when he was 12 years old. He opened up to my mother, much to my amazement. I didn't care about their conversations, and left the room to leave them alone. Their conversations were so intimate, I felt I was an intruder. I recalled the year when she didn't leave her bed for the entire time Dad was in Mexico to avoid the draft, so this investment in keeping Mom "happy" was survival for me and the family.

Joe never talked about his mother's death. I discovered the events leading up to her death from his Aunt Maria. We would talk for hours about life, history and everything I wanted to know about Joe, because Joe didn't talk to me about anything. She told me they had found Joe's mother, Despina, dead in front of their house. A neighbor brought her body upstairs, and put her on a table. According to Greek customs, his family wanted Joe to bond with his mother, even in death. He stayed by her side for an entire night. This traumatic event left him with a serious demeanor as before-and-after pictures demonstrate. That dazzling smile of his would return when he was around his sport playing buddies, or with others he felt comfortable with, but never me. I used to watch him smile with my mother. With me, however, that smile was nowhere to be found.

Despite his silence, Joe and I were inseparable. Because I had given myself to him sexually, I felt I had to marry him. My parents had drilled this idea deep into me. We didn't talk about it since we never talked about anything intimate. Joe was so friendly with everyone except me. I just accepted it. He was on the varsity basketball team, and he knew everything about sports. That was our connection. I was proud to be with Mr. Popularity of his senior class, with that million dollar smile.

In 1952, Joe graduated from high school and was drafted into the army. Luckily, he was stationed not far from San Francisco, so we saw each other on the weekends. In 1953, my father moved us to San Mateo so I spent my junior year commuting to San Francisco. I did not like the hour-and-a-half commute. In my senior year, I transferred to San Mateo High School. That was to be the greatest year of my high school life.

At San Mateo High, I met a group of outrageous senior girls who liked me because they were attracted to Joe. There were three of them: Jackie, Joyce, and Judy. We were inseparable, and I was happy to have new friends. Every Friday night we would go up into the mountains of San Mateo to drink beer, run around naked, and jump into a pond screaming with joy. We began shoplifting, going into stores and putting things on under our clothes. We were four hoodlums even though they were from affluent families and had never behaved that way before. They were showing off for me.

It was a fun year, but the most memorable person for me was an English teacher, Miss Cook, who taught Shakespeare and many other classical pieces of literature. I loved her passion, and I soon became engrossed in literature. Shakespeare, Chaucer, and other writers fascinated me. Miss Cook taught me that great teachers have great passion.

When graduation came, I was sad as I had had such incredible fun with my three new friends. Joe was now stationed in Louisville, Kentucky, and I knew I would be marrying him soon and moving there. I wanted to get away from home and discover the world. I was depressed to leave my friends and I went to my graduation drunk. I hated leaving my new friends.

Chapter 15, My Big Fat Greek Wedding

When I was 18, three days after I graduated high school in 1954, I had the wedding of a lifetime. I was totally withdrawn going through all the planning of this huge wedding since Joe's grandmother, Lala, and his Aunt Marie planned the entire affair as is the custom on the island of Crete, Greece. The only thing the bride is required to provide is a big dowry, which I did not have. What I offered was myself. That apparently was enough as Joe's family all loved me because I was fun and made them laugh. One has to learn Greek dances to have a big Greek wedding, and my love for dance made this easy.

Joe's father, Costos, appeared two weeks before the wedding, and I was taken with him immediately. We became close right away and loved to be with each other. He was so handsome, with a big smile, white hair and a personality that was nothing but fun. A movie scout had brought him from Crete to Hollywood in 1940 to play Rudolph Valentino's double in films. Unfortunately, Rudolph died a year later. Costos came to visit friends in San Francisco and met Joe's mother. They got married. Costos wanted to move back to Hollywood after a few years in San Francisco. Joe's mother, Despina, did not want to live in Hollywood, so they fought a lot. Joe was born into this chaos. After a few years, Costos left and went off to live in Hollywood. He rarely visited Joe and this turned Joe's feelings sour towards his father.

Before the wedding, Joe's father bought me many clothes. His lucrative professions as a hair stylist and real estate broker made him financially well off. No one had ever pampered me in this way by buying me so many clothes. Such an indulgence! I was overwhelmed by all the gifts.

I really loved Costos because of the fun we had together. We would laugh the entire time we spent in each other's company. He was a charmer, and I just wanted to run off with him. Never had I met such a sophisticated and generous man before. People told me I was very similar to Joe's deceased mother, so maybe that's why both Joe and his father were so taken by me.

All I could think about was Costos; he captivated me. I was torn: I was marrying Joe, but loved his father. I did not want to marry Joe, but because of the fact that we had sex — there was no question in my mind. I *had* to marry him if we had sex, like a good Catholic girl. I felt no protest to the norm, all I could feel was sadness. This is another example of how I abandoned myself and followed the dictates of society and the Church rather than listen to myself.

The night before the wedding, I descended the stairs to sleep in my usual place. There was no room upstairs in the old Victorian house for me to sleep. I slept in the backseat of Joe's grandfather's 1936 Nash Roadster. The car sat parked in the downstairs garage at Joe's house. The car had a massive and comfortable back seat the length of my body; it was a pleasure to sleep in it. No one except Joe knew I was there. Since my parents moved to their new home in San Mateo, I felt it was too far to drive there from San Francisco on my wedding day. My father was too busy chasing women and wouldn't take the time to drive me to the city in time for me to prepare for the wedding.

On our wedding day, June 20th, 1954, Joe and I were playing catch football outside his home. *Who plays football on their wedding day?* This was where we both felt comfortable, connecting and communicating through sports. That was the primary focus of our relationship: playing sports, going to sporting events, dancing, and having sex. There was no verbal communication, no exchange of feelings, it was all about doing. However, I was desperate to leave my home and escape my father's lust-filled eyes. My skin would crawl, and I wanted to get as far away as possible. I never realized the price I would pay.

On that day in June, the sun had broken through the clouds and the temperature rose as I became hot and sweaty. I quickly took a sponge bath as the time was approaching for our wedding. I felt more comfortable and loved at Joe's house than I did at mine. I was embraced, appreciated and loved by this warm Greek family. It was such a contrast to the cold, distant and rejecting behavior exhibited by my mother.

When we arrived at the church full of guests, all I could do was look for Costos. His big smile made me realize I had chosen the wrong man to marry. I began to cry, part of me realizing I was abandoning myself again. Joe and I paraded around the altar as the priest swung the incense burner chanting prayers for us. My attention was totally on Costos.

The big surprise came after the church ceremony when we went to Moose Hall, a huge hall in downtown San Francisco. I was so shocked when I saw it was packed full of people. I didn't know who had been invited as Marie, Joe's aunt, had dealt with all the invitations. George Christopher, the mayor of San Francisco, was there with his wife who had gone to school with Joe's mother. People had come from all over the country. Greek weddings are always very big. They go all out to show their best. Gold necklaces and bracelets were given to me in abundance! They were bright and shiny but held no meaning for me.

My father looked so handsome in his white tuxedo. My bridesmaids from high school were enamored with him; and, as usual, he tried to make out with them at the reception. Somehow that didn't surprise me. My father was a Casanova. Mom remained in denial as she always did. True to her Catholic upbringing, she ignored his indiscretions.

The food was memorable, but the best part of the wedding was the Greek dancing. Everyone loved it, and all my family tried to dance. The reception lasted for six hours, and Joe and I were the last to leave. We had such a great time! I was depressed when it was over as I knew the next day we would be driving across the country to Louisville, Kentucky, where Joe was stationed at Fort Knox.

The climax of the evening happened when we went to the hotel where we were to spend our wedding night and found a room full of gorgeous flowers. On the bed were two lovely silk nightgowns and a silk dressing gown. They were from Costos. I felt like a princess. I was so taken by his incredible gifts. Costos was responsible for this magical room. It seemed like a dream. But the quick fuck from Joe before passing out brought me back to reality.

The dream ended the next morning when we began the long drive across the country. I looked forward to traveling, in fact that was the most important reason why I married Joe. Oh yes, and getting away from my father's leering eyes.

Chapter 16, My Year in Louisville, Kentucky

The long drive from San Francisco to Louisville, Kentucky, took four days and three nights. I was sick the entire time from the heat and riding with a man who was unable to carry on a conversation. There were no other people to interact with—just Joe and me. I immediately felt depressed and regretted having married Joe. I settled into resignation. I had married him and that was it. There was no turning back. I had watched my mother slip into depression and I was unconsciously mirroring her behavior. We arrived in Louisville.

I asked Joe, "Where is the apartment you rented for us?"

"It fell through."

"Why didn't you tell me?" I asked. Since I had moved every year with my family, this was no big deal, I knew we would find a place and not be homeless.

"I forgot," he responded, sheepishly.

The next morning after leaving the motel, we found a big room available which I loved. The imposing tall Victorian doors and windows brought a sense of spaciousness. The high ceiling, and a lovely garden with flowers of every color felt so much like the South that I had seen in the movies. I was content even if Joe was moody and did not talk to me.

I believed Joe was having an affair because he would come home late two nights a week. I knew he was hiding something from me, but I could not put my finger on it. He was acting strangely and he wouldn't talk about it. He would come up with some excuse about having to work late. After two months of this behavior, my anger and fear demanded he tell me where he was spending his time on Tuesday and Thursday nights. He confessed, "I've been going to a place trying to get my balding head to grow hair."

The following week, I had a flat tire outside the front of our house. I asked a black man passing by if he could help me fix my flat tire. He said, "Of course." I was grateful but had no money to pay him, so I asked him if he would like a cold glass of lemonade. He said, "Yes, thank you." I invited him into our place and he said, "Are you sure?"

I said, "Of course."

The next day the landlady knocked on our door and along with a racial slur, said we could not live in her place because a black man had been in my room. I objected but all she could say was, "You need to find another place."

I was stunned, but that was to be just the first of many shocking incidents I would encounter in the South. For instance, I sat in the "wrong" part of the bus and went to the "wrong" bathroom—both places for black folks, not "white people." Being from San Francisco, I never really understood racism, it is so utterly evil.

We found a lovely two bedroom apartment on the other side of Louisville, which I liked better. There was even a swimming pool down the street from our house. I had never experienced humidity before, or thunder and lightning storms, which occurred often. I remember being told I had to get out of the swimming pool when there was a lightning storm, and I did not want to. It was so much fun seeing the lightning and hearing the blasting of the thunder.

There was also a big park down the street that had a dance floor. I sneaked over there on Sundays and watched men dancing with each other and women dancing with women. I could not believe my eyes. I had never seen such a thing in California; and here it was just considered normal, and out of all places it was in Louisville, Kentucky. I was fascinated and excited, shocked to see them—I felt I belonged there. I wanted to dance with a woman, but I was too shy to ask.

After a few months I longed to return home. I was so unhappy with Joe who would never talk to me. We watched TV, ate, slept, and had sex. That was our life.

I decided to leave him and go back to California by bus. But as fate would have it, I fainted at a bus stop and after seeing a doctor I found out that I was pregnant. My Dad had told me not to come home pregnant, so going back to Joe was my only option. Joe never even knew I had tried to leave him, so life in Kentucky continued.

Costos wrote me one letter, but he had a hard time expressing himself in writing. I felt extremely lonely and watching soap operas in the morning, eating potato chips, and drinking Pepsi was my morning routine. In the afternoon, I would go swimming and read science fiction books. A few months into the pregnancy, I suddenly felt none of the emotions that were bringing me down. Nothing bothered me; I had never felt so peaceful. No anxiety, premenstrual cramps, or heavy periods—just a feeling of well-being came over me for the next six months. I became a contented pregnant cow.

Joe went down to Georgia for special training. He would write to me on long pieces of toilet paper, he expressed his love for me in such a memorable manner. I use to wish he would go off and write to me so I could feel his love as he never expressed it when we were together.

Bill, Joe's army buddy, and his wife Lorraine entered our lives. They moved into our extra bedroom. It was fun to have a friend to talk to. Lorraine wanted to be pregnant and they had tried for years. I felt sad for her but jealous too because Bill was a warm, loving man. We played cards every night, laughing and talking. It was fun for three months. Then Bill was discharged from the army, and they returned to their hometown of Chicago.

I wanted to visit them so we took the long drive one weekend. Chicago fascinated me with its huge buildings, black from the coal they used for heating. People were friendly, but different. They expressed how they felt about things. I had picked up a Southern drawl, so they were shocked when I told them I was from San Francisco. We went to bars—this was the first time I'd ever been to one. Getting drunk there on two beers further cemented that drinking was good to numb pain. Even so, I did not begin to drink heavily until the 1980s.

When April arrived, I knew I was going to have my baby soon as the pressure in my abdomen became quite intense. Then, on April 4th in the cold of the night, we took the long, sixty-mile drive from Louisville to Fort Knox Army Hospital where I was to deliver at five o'clock in the morning on the 5th of April. After six painful hours of labor, I gave birth to my first daughter who we named after Joe's mother, Despina. She came into the world screaming, and she did not stop for two weeks. I thought I had given birth to a monster, and I did not know what to do with her.

Every night for the week I stayed in the hospital, the nurses would wheel all the babies into the ward, and I would hear Despina screaming. She would suck on my breasts, chewing with such intensity that my breasts began to bleed. No one gave me any instructions on how to handle her, and I went home from the hospital not knowing what to do. After a week of not sleeping from Despina screaming, I returned to the hospital. The doctor there decided she might be allergic to my milk, so they suggested I try goat's milk. I was grateful that after two weeks of her screaming she found satisfaction with goat's milk. Finally, she began to sleep.

Our life changed. Despina became my object of attention. Joe never was that comfortable with her. He had wanted a son, but he tried to be helpful. I think the experience with his mother passing at a young age affected him deeply, having to sit all night next to her dead body just because of a Greek custom. I feel this horrible trauma affected him his entire life, and how he responded to Despina entering our lives. I never saw him cry, he was totally shut down—sometimes after an emotional film he would watch me cry and have no reaction.

We made new friends, and for the next two months I was content with being a mom and looking forward to returning home to San Francisco. June 20, our anniversary, was the day that Joe would be discharged from the Army.

The long drive back was fun. We were both very happy to be going home, and Despina basked in that joy. On the drive back, she was lying on her stomach and held her head up for the first time with a big smile on her face, it was a memorable moment.

We stopped in Hollywood to see Joe's father as he wanted to show us his big surprise. When we arrived, all my old feelings had sort of disappeared as he and I had no real communication that year. Costos was excited to show us the new house he had built for us to live in. It even had a swimming pool. Joe told him he did not want to live in Southern California, and Costos appeared immensely sad. We had to leave even though he was so disheartened. I felt sad, too, but anxious to get back to my home in San Francisco. Later we heard that Costos had returned to Greece to find a woman to marry. He succeeded and eventually had four children with her, he was almost sixty. They lived in the house he had built for us, with his new family until he died 26 years later from a heart attack.

I was so happy to be back home in San Francisco and see all my family. My sister Dottie adored Despina, and Joe started to come out of himself. He too was happy to be home. I appreciated my beloved San Francisco more than ever for its diversity and beauty unlike any other city I had known.

Being back was great for a while. I loved Joe's big family as they loved me and showered me with a great deal of attention and appreciation—especially Joe's aunt, Marie. I loved her greatly, she was a brilliant woman. We continued our lengthy discussions for hours, about life, travel, and education; and this was my first encounter with an intellectual woman. I loved our discussions and would look forward to the Sunday night dinners at Joe's grandmother Lala's house. The whole family would talk about politics in this country and in Greece. I then realized I wanted to go to college.

Chapter 17, Despina - My Brilliant, Eccentric Daughter

I became pregnant with Despina three weeks after I married Joe. Our withdrawal from birth control started once we were legally married even though I wasn't ready to have children at 19.

My pregnancy was made bearable through my diet of Pepsi Cola and potato chips. They were my comfort foods. I felt like a contented cow, though I had no maternal instincts. I did not want to be pregnant, but I knew nothing about abortion.

Despina was born in Fort Knox, Kentucky, on April 5, 1955, in an army hospital. I received no education for what to expect, I was totally ignorant. There was no prenatal care, and the first time I saw my doctor was when he delivered my baby. The six hours of labor were very intense, and I went through it totally alone. When the nurses would wheel the babies out into the huge room of thirty beds, I would always hear Despina screaming. When she was switched from breast milk to goat's milk, her screaming came to a halt.

Despina's first trauma came when she was two years old. She swallowed an opened safety pin. Thank goodness her little friend came and told me. On the way to the hospital, Joe said to me, "She'd better not die, or you will follow." He had spoken like a true Greek: an eye for an eye.

As soon as we arrived, the doctors had to cut Despina's stomach open. Of course she spent the night there, but in those days parents didn't stay with their children overnight in hospitals. The next day, we rushed back to the hospital anxiously. There was Despina walking around the hospital wheeling a big pole that held her IV. I thought she would still be in her bed and was shocked and overjoyed with such a rapid recovery.

Despina was a character from day one as she loved to sing, dance, and entertain. She would create talent shows and put on performances for all the family, but it didn't stop with the family. We went to Disneyland when she was three years old. All of sudden, we could not find her. After a frantic search for her, we found her leading the Disneyland band!

She learned how to swim on her own at age five. She loved the water, and we spent a great deal of time on the beach. When she entered Kindergarten, problems began. She could not sit still, and I was frequently going to school to see the teacher about my daughter's behavior issues. This continued until she was 7 years old when she joined the San Francisco Children's Opera. Her behavior changed because I told her she had to behave in school if she wanted to go to the children's opera. She became a star immediately as she loved to be on the stage performing.

Despina has told me, as an adult, that she put much of her energy into trying to keep her father and I together. When she failed, she felt it so deeply that it changed her life tremendously as her agony began with Joe not in our home. She was seven when we divorced.

In junior high school, Despina's behavior changed again when she and her sister, Roxanne, discovered drugs. This was the beginning of a nightmare for me. It was the late 60s, and drugs, sex and rock and roll were everywhere, especially in San Francisco. She entered George Washington High School where I was teaching. Right away, she got involved with a young black boy, and the black girls would gang up on her and threatened to hurt her physically. I decided I had to transfer her to another school as I was afraid for her life. Somehow she managed to graduate, but she was now a very quiet young lady.

It was around this time that my sister had begun chanting Nam Myoho Renge Kyo, the practice of Nichiren Buddhism. Though initially I was skeptical, her transformation due to her spiritual practice had her released from the mental hospital. I thought I would try chanting to find some peace in my life, especially with my out of control daughters. I first chanted to prove that Buddhists were crazy. I began to see the result of the "actual proof" of chanting in my life. The fear that sat within me my entire life was suddenly lessened by a growing confidence. With the way my daughters were acting in their teens and the amount of drugs around, I chanted for them—and myself—to survive.

The next summer, I took my girls to Europe for the second time. We traveled all over. Then, when she was 18, Despina moved into her own apartment in the Presidio. She turned her apartment into a house of prostitution and her younger sister joined her. Despina told me not to worry, she knew what she was doing. They only serviced Japanese men, she said, as they were easy according to her. Roxanne was 15, and when I discovered her involvement in the prostitution, I had her put in Juvenile Hall. Despina was of age, so I had no control over her life. I felt helpless. It didn't help Roxanne either as she was a drug addict like Despina.

A few years later after attempting to get off heroin, Despina entered an 8 month long live in a therapeutic community and stayed off of heroin. A few months after graduating from it, she was back on it so she left for Europe to get away from the drug saturated environment of San Francisco, taking her sister Roxanne with her. Unfortunately, they discovered opium from the local Arabs while in the Middle East. Then they went to Paris to get jobs as au pairs. Despina had begun chanting, and focused her prayer on getting the best job. She got a great job with a very wealthy family and also joined a group that sang in nightclubs.

Roxanne returned home after a few months as she did not like the job she found in Paris. When Despina finally arrived back in the U.S. a year later, she found her old boyfriend, Tony, had begun a relationship with Roxanne. Tony wanted to get Roxanne off drugs, but he didn't succeed. Instead, they all began using drugs together. When Despina returned home, she was devastated with her sister betraying her. She was still in love with Tony. Even so, she joined the two of them in New York after Tony took Roxanne there, when she turned 18. The girls worked in peep shows in New York to make money. I went to see them once, and they were on stage making love to each other. I found it very sensual, but I did not like the vulgar environment with men gazing at them.

What is amazing about my daughter Despina is that she had signed up to go to Guyana with Jim Jones and at the last minute decided to go to New York. This was two months before the tragedy in Jonestown took place, and she would have been one of 900 who drank the Kool aid and died.

Despina's involvement with drugs continued for years. When she was in her late 20s, Despina decided she wanted to have children. She returned to San Francisco, got clean, sober, and healthy. Her love life had mostly been with black men, but out of nowhere Ted Douglas appeared. I had met him one day at a Buddhist meeting and thought: *Why can't my daughter be with a Buddhist like him?* He was a practicing Buddhist without a drug problem, gainfully employed, and healthy. He was the straightest man she had dated and that surprised me. Despina had practiced Buddhism on and off for many years, but her drug problem always got in her way. Then, after 3 years of being clean and sober, Despina came home and told me she was pregnant. Due to a health issue, she had been told that she would never get pregnant, so we were delighted with the news of her pregnancy. She was pregnant and off of drugs. Her life had turned around, but not her sister's. When Ted walked into our house, I was shocked because I had wished for this to happen and it was unfolding right before my eyes.

Despina now has two fantastic, talented sons who also practice Buddhism and are successful in their chosen fields. Miles, the oldest, was named after Miles Davis and also shares his birthday with Herbie Hancock. It's mystical because he is quite happy as a music producer and a piano player. Zachary, her second son, recently graduated from UC Berkeley and is pursuing a career in food politics.

Despina is the best mother I have ever seen. She has the wisdom, love, and patience that constantly amazes me. I am so grateful that she is still alive.

Chapter 18, Roxanne, My Greek Tragedy

Roxanne was born October 1, 1957. I was still reluctantly married to the emotionally unavailable Joe. Running and surfing to quiet my frustrations of being married to a man that did not communicate helped me to feel some relief. Even after having two children, undisclosed to anyone and hidden from myself was my secret desire to be with a woman.

Roxanne was born with deformed legs. I felt responsible because I never wanted to be pregnant. The guilt around her defect followed both Joe and I around throughout her life like a heavy burden of remorse we couldn't shake. It was all that church shit coming back to haunt me. The priest told me not to use birth control, that God would take care of me and I foolishly listened. I dropped out of the Catholic religion after that.

The doctors put Roxanne in braces when she was six months old, and all she did was cry. My friend, Annie, took us to her Russian doctor who took off the braces, advising us to do specific exercises three times a day for her legs. Eventually, he suggested we walk and run on the beach as the sand would facilitate the development of her muscles. He gave her a diet of homemade yogurt, steamed vegetables, fresh fruit, and brown rice. After three months, her legs were straight. Our picture even made the San Francisco Chronicle: Roxanne and I running the beach at 7 o'clock in the morning. What a way to begin the day.

Joe and I were locked in a constant battle. I wanted a relationship with him, but he continued to be unavailable and his favorite phrase was, "I don't know!" We tried therapy with a man who reminded me of Joe. I wasn't invested in the counseling because I had already made up my mind that I wanted to be with a woman.

Roxanne and her father were inseparable, not like her sister, Despina who was deemed too needy by Joe. By the time Roxanne was four years old, I could no longer remain married. I had finally asked Joe to leave after our one and only session with the therapist. Roxanne was devastated when he left. She asked me, "Is Daddy coming home?" I was shocked by her display of emotion. My self absorption at 23 was so deep that I had no awareness of my children's feelings. How was I to know about emotions, I had literally run away from them all my life. Her face was full of pain laboring under the emotion but not understanding what the adults in her life were doing.

Joe remarried soon after our divorce to a woman who had two daughters. These girls were constantly beaten for misconduct, but my girls never shared that information. This was to have a horrible effect on Roxanne as she was not punished and felt guilty because she partook in the mischievous behavior with her stepsisters.

Roxanne's devastation of her father's leaving began to be apparent at her first day of Kindergarten. I had dropped her off with her sister in the morning. When I went to pick her up, she was not there. I ran home frantically, but could not find her. Finally, I heard a voice in the cellar, and there she was. I asked, "Why did you leave school?" nIt was all I could do to control my feelings.

She answered, "I don't know anyone." This was what I had done at the same age when I was in Kindergarten: ran home.

After I encouraged her, she returned to school unhappily. At the end of the year, when she was to be promoted, the teacher told me she did not feel Roxanne was ready for first grade.

I asked, "Why?"

She said, "Roxanne will not socialize, and she will not recite her ABCs out loud."

So with much encouragement, she returned to school the next day, recited her ABCs, and was able to move on to the next grade. But the same problem occurred in the first grade. She would not read out loud until the teacher told her she would not be promoted. Only then did she unwillingly read.

Roxanne was a very talented child. When she would sing, mimicking Despina, we would all be amused with her humor. She was a good painter, dancer, and a great athlete. When she entered junior high school, she won a prize in a poetry contest of the San Francisco Chronicle. She had written a moving poem about Martin Luther King, Jr. who had just been shot.

Even though she was so talented, Roxanne was in a lot of emotional and physical pain. I noticed when she became depressed and wanted to be alone. These mood swings brought me out of my self absorption long enough to realize she was going through something. However, I was so overextended by going to college and working, that there was little emotional energy left for my girls. Roxanne stopped doing her physical exercises at home and when I asked her why, she would say, "Mom, I did them in school."

In 7th grade, I noticed she was sleeping more but that was because she began abusing drugs. Drugs were easy to buy as other kids were selling them at school. She discovered drugs could numb her pain. Her personality changed. She became more outgoing until she got into heroin. I found her constantly nodding out. Drug programs did not work for her because she really did not want to stop using. She and her sister were in at least three rehab facilities. Roxanne would always run away and go and live with another addict.

San Francisco in the 70s was a city in which the flower children had taken over with their drugs, rock and roll, and sex. It was vibrantly alive with peace demonstrations against the Vietnam war, African Americans demanding their rights, gays wanting to be out and in the open; you name it, it was happening in San Francisco.

Roxanne never finished high school. She quit in her junior year. Soon after we went to Europe, and there, with my daughters' unsuccessful attempt at kicking drugs and subsequent introduction to opium, it was clear her drug addiction was claiming more and more of her life. After a few months in Paris, Roxanne returned to San Francisco and started going out with Despina's boyfriend, Tony. He was a drug counselor and wanted to get Roxanne clean. Eventually, Tony had to return to New York and took Roxanne, feeling she needed to get away from all the addicts in San Francisco. Needless to say, she found them in New York just as easily. When Despina came home from Paris, she was devastated that her sister had gone off with her boyfriend. But Tony began to call Despina every night as he was worried about Roxanne and needed her help. Despina decided to move to New York.

Roxanne was constantly disappearing and running off with other addicts. I once flew desperately to New York to find her as she had disappeared for a week. Tony and I found her in a house where she was shooting up heroin. It was the most frightening place I had ever been in my life. I was horrified to see so many people lying around looking half dead. The energy was the feeling of death. Besides being filthy, the walls were all cracked with empty cans and bottles lying on the floor in such disarray. I fled the place alone feeling so helpless. Running made it so that I could alter my state to survive until I found my Buddhist practice. Roxanne was completely lost in the drug world.

Despina left New York after several years, but Roxanne remained there for another decade. Finally, Tony could no longer stand being with a drug addict, and he sent her back to San Francisco. When Despina and I went to pick her up at the airport, I was stunned to see how haggard Roxanne had become from her addiction. Her skin was ashen grey, eyes blood shot, her gorgeous smile was no longer bright and full of love as it once had made everyone love her. I just wanted to take her home and fix her so she could get well. My denial of my inability to help her was also part of the problem. I really thought I could help, especially after she would promise she wanted to change. I gave her the room in the back of my house for her to live in.

After a few months she stopped using drugs and decided she wanted to get her own place. She had found a policeman who fell in love with her, Johnny. Johnny and Roxanne were together for three years and then she began using drugs again. She just could not stay in a drug program long enough to get the tools she needed for recovery.

I took her home with me once again as she was sick with the deteriorating illness of addiction. She was thirty years old and very depressed. The only pleasure she had was being with Despina's son, Miles. She would give him one m&m's candy each time he would make her laugh. They had wonderful times together. Roxanne loved children and wanted to have her own. She had had five abortions not wanting to have a child born a drug addict. By the time she was 34, she became even more depressed. I relied heavily on my Buddhist practice of chanting to see me through her changes.

All her cousins, friends, and stepsisters had gotten married. She was basically alone. She disappeared for a few days, and I was frantically looking for her, chanting and chanting but was unable to find her.

Then out of nowhere in July 18, 1993, I got a call from my daughter Despina telling me Roxanne was nowhere to be found and she was supposed to be with her boyfriend Johnny. Despina was staying at my home in Healdsburg, and I was in our house on Jamestown Street in San Francisco. All I could do was sit in front of the Gohonzon and chant. All of a sudden I had this need to go downstairs into our garage. Roxanne had taped all the air holes. I pulled up the door and there sat Roxanne's car. Full of fear, frozen with anxiety, I walked over to the car and opened the front door— there laid my beautiful Roxanne. I could not believe the peace surrounding her face. She had taken her life. I went into an altered state of existence as I slowly removed her gold necklace that I wear to this day. I had not seen her look so beautiful in such a long time. Drug abuse had made her life impossible to continue, even though she had gone through many drug programs, always leaving them after a few weeks.

In my altered state, I called the police and had her body taken away. My niece Lorraine came over crying, and I could only hug her. Ted, my son-in-law, had to plan the memorial, I was not functioning. I returned to my home on the Russian River, where I finally broke down and cried and continued crying and chanting for ten days, and ten nights. Then out of nowhere on the tenth sleepless night, a meteorite ran across the big window of my house on the river. All of a sudden, I felt her spirit enter my body and I stopped crying because I felt her within me and she has never left. I knew then the power of Nam Myoho Renge Kyo, which is the devotion of the mystic law of cause and effect, that life and death are one. Ever since, I have been a very devoted Buddhist, introducing many people who are suffering to this practice of Buddhism.

I had another mystical experience, days later when we went to the Bay across the street from Candlestick Park on the pier in San Francisco. I threw her ashes into the water when a gust of wind came up out of nowhere and her ashes spread out all over me. I immediately started acting like Roxanne, singing and dancing. I became her, it was an unreal experience that made me believe in the spiritual world in a most profound manner.

I was not a very good mother. I didn't know how to take care of my children. I repeated my mother's pattern, although totally unaware I was doing it. My children had the misfortune to pick me as their mother. I did not know how to be a mother because no one had mothered me. We all suffered greatly as a result. I knew something big was missing in my life and had no idea what that was.

Chapter 19, Annie

I have had so many lovers, I can't even remember them all. My childhood was deprived of the nurturing love I saw my brothers receive from my parents. There remained an empty void I desperately tried to fill with sex. I was a love addict, looking for love outside myself. By choosing unavailable people, just like my parents, I searched and searched but never found the love I craved. I ignored my daughters' emotional needs not knowing how to give the affection that was absent in my life. My focus was to have a lover, no matter what price I had to pay. I dated several alcoholics and would drink intensely after each relationship ended. I couldn't drink while I was with them, however, because I had to take care of them. My loneliness returned and it drove me on to the next lover, and the next, and the next.

After moving back to San Francisco from Kentucky, we lived in Joe's grandmother's apartment. I was 20 years old, a stay-at-home, bored, out to lunch, ignorant youth with a toddler that I had no idea how to care for. I was miserable being married and looked for any escape from my desperation. Watching mindless soap operas, eating potato chips, and drinking soda was again my daily escape from reality. My sister, Dottie, arrived early one morning at my home. She was excited as she wanted me to meet her new friend, Annie. Dottie said to me, "Ruth, what has happened to you? You are not like your old wild and playful self. You have grown fat. Come on out to the beach with me. It's a shame what has happened to you."

I respected my sister's advice as she had changed her own life so dramatically from being a sickly child to a healthy, vibrant young woman. Her enthusiasm was infectious, and her new friend Annie sounded very interesting.

The first time I saw Annie she was standing on the stairs that led down to the beach. I was shocked when I watched her fighting with an angry old man. "You dirty Bolshevik Communist! Go back to Russia where you came from!" he shouted at her.

"You're nothing but a Capitalist Pig!" she responded.

I looked at her, aghast! Here was the first woman I saw outwardly and loudly expressing her feelings. I wanted to know her, she had the courage to be herself. She was the external manifestation of my innermost secret desires. She took my breath away. She was from Russia, short and stout with blondish grey hair and warm, piercing blue eyes. I felt she could see through me the moment she looked at me. She had a limp, but that only gave her a greater presence. She walked as if she owned the world. Her skin was wrinkled and worn from too much sun but that did nothing to detract from her essence.

Annie was always speaking out against the raging McCarthyism that was going on in the 50s. I was politically ignorant but could see her logic behind the evils of Capitalism. I wanted to know more, so she took me to several communist meetings. I became increasingly more interested in politics.

Whenever we were not going to communist meetings, she would take me to foreign movies or classical concerts. I would sit next to her, blissed out by Beethoven and the smell of garlic emanating from her breath. Annie opened up the world of literature to me. Tolstoy, Pushkin, and Dostoevsky were my favorites. Annie enjoyed reading to me, something I had never had as a child except from my sister Dottie. Annie infused the stories I read with her unique perspective and intonations. Her excitement was contagious. I had never seen such passion in any other person before. As an extremely emotional woman, she would cry and laugh easily. She was full of life. What a contrast from my cold, emotionally numb parents and husband.

I was totally captivated by her personality and her enthusiasm about everything. She loved our daughters, Dottie's Lana and my Despina. She would romp and play with the children for hours, thoroughly enjoying them, making sand castles and playing in the water. Everyday I would get up early, clean the house, prepare the food for the day and run to see her. I was so happy with my new friend and my ability to carry on a conversation.

I attempted to carry on a conversation with Joe. I wanted to try, after all I was thinking it was my fault that he was so silent. I would ask him what he was thinking, and he continued to say, "Nothing."

"What are you feeling?"

"Nothing."

I was married to "nothing." He read the sports section of the paper, watched the TV, and listened to the radio all at the same time. His entire world revolved around sports, not around me or our daughters.

Annie immigrated to the US in the 1930s from Russia with her husband, Samuel, who later died of cancer. She had a son, David, who married an orthodox Jewish woman. His wife hated Annie's being a communist. Annie could not visit her son in New York for this reason. David, however, visited Annie every year. They would have big fights about his wife's attitude toward Annie.

Annie expressed how happy she was to have us as her new family. The first year of our relationship was wonderful. Then, in what seemed to come out of nowhere, I started to feel physically attracted to Annie; and I didn't know what to do with it. I was 21 years old and Annie was 62. I could not speak to anyone about my feelings, which made me feel even more confused. At that time in the late 1950s, homosexuality was never talked about so I felt scared. To feel sane again, I would surf in the ocean or run on the beach. Then I became pregnant so that Despina could have a brother or sister.

Pregnancy quieted my outrageous sexual feelings, and due to the pregnancy, Annie showered attention on me. I felt loved and adored by her. She was so happy I was having another child. She made special food for me and always talked about the new baby as if it were going to be hers. When I gave birth to Roxanne, Annie was there by my side. All I could think of was how much I loved her. One night, in her apartment, I started to make love to her. She laughed in my face! I never felt so humiliated in my life. After that, our relationship changed.

As I said before, Roxanne was born with a deformity, but it was Annie's doctor who had suggested the exercises that helped her. My life was divided: weekdays with Annie and weekends with Joe and his family. I still had no place in which to resolve those haunting, sexual feelings for her.

Annie and I went on a two week vacation to the Russian River. One morning, I awoke with the thought of making love to her. Knowing it was impossible made me want to move on with my life.

I was then to meet Annie's friend, Esther. When I met Esther, she asked me how I felt about psychiatrists. I said I thought they were all crazy. As I didn't know better, Esther was a psychiatrist, and she would not tell me her profession! She and I would walk each day for an hour while Annie took care of the children. I didn't know it, but Esther was psychoanalyzing me. Annie was extremely jealous and soon our beautiful relationship became very painful. I could no longer take her jealous outbursts. I would see her on the beach, and she wouldn't talk to me. Sometimes she would say insulting things. She called Esther a thief as she felt Esther took me away from her. Eventually Annie became ill with cancer. Dottie visited her regularly. Annie's dream was to go back to Russia to live her last days in the country she loved, and that she did. She took her last breath on the ship returning to Russia, alone.

Chapter 20, Esther

I became increasingly more frustrated with Annie. I wanted to connect with her sexually but I had been shunned. As I became sick of my feelings for Annie, I needed help with my frustrations, yet I was completely unaware of that need. Interestingly, the universe took care of me in a subtle way as Esther was to make me aware of my feelings.

The first time I met her, she said to Annie, "Where did you find this beautiful woman?" No one had ever talked about me that way before. I was shocked when she looked at me with such admiring eyes. Of course, I was impressed. Someone was actually verbalizing appreciation for me. Naturally, I wanted to know this woman who was short and not beautiful, but handsome with a keen way of expressing herself. She was also from Russia, an intellectual woman who fascinated me.

Esther immediately asked me if I would like to join her on a walk along the beach. It was a warm sunny day in 1958, and I felt somewhat honored that this intelligent woman wanted to get to know me. Men had always been attracted to me, but never such a sophisticated woman. Esther was 50 years old. I was 22 and naive. I could not believe I was able to keep up an intelligent conversation with this woman.

Esther had come from Russia when she was 30 years old. She spoke perfect English while Annie had such a heavy Russian accent. Esther enunciated her words beautifully. I loved to hear her speak the English language. Esther was as equally intrigued by me and wanted to know more about me. No one else had ever expressed an interest in getting to know me like Esther did. I was shocked but found it easy to talk to her. We would walk twice a week on the San Francisco beach and talk for an hour. I longed to see her each week as her questions fascinated me. Because I had told her that I thought psychiatrists were crazy, she told me she was a businesswoman. There was no more discussion about her work after that.

All the feelings I had for Annie immediately transferred to Esther, and I began to fall in love with her. Each Tuesday and Thursday, I would wake up excited as these were the days I would see Esther for our hour long walk on the beach. I was happy again; and Joe, my husband, was pleased that I had found a new friend.

Esther took me to my first opera. I was overwhelmed with the power of the singers as I had never heard opera before. I came from a working-class family. The only singing I had heard was the choir in the Catholic church. The world of opera had a class of people I had never been exposed to before. I was impressed and so grateful to go to all the operas with Esther. I loved the way she would have conversations with people. She was a curious, charismatic woman who charmed everyone she talked to, including me. I just gazed in wonder when she had conversations with other people. She was warm and engaging, always smiling; a true Leo.

Esther was only serious when she questioned me about my life. Then the conversation became quite intense though I did not know at the time, that she was psychoanalyzing me. I really began to think about my feelings as Esther would always ask me how I felt about everything. I had never experienced that before. I felt acknowledged for the first time in my life. It was such a good feeling. I could not get enough. I wanted to spend more time with Esther, but she had a very busy life. After a year of our friendship, I asked Esther if she would like to go to Santa Cruz with me for a weekend. She was delighted. When I went to pick her up, I got extremely frightened. I realized I wanted something from Esther that I could not ask from her. I wanted to go to bed with this woman, and I was scared. On the drive to Santa Cruz I almost ran off the road twice. I was so frightened, but Esther just laughed at me. Nothing was discussed about my feelings.

When we arrived in Santa Cruz, I told Esther I was sick and needed to go back home. I could not talk about my true feelings, and we went back to San Francisco. After that, our meetings became painful.

All I remember from that time was Esther's saying she wanted to go to see the Bolshoi Russian Ballet but could not wait in line all day for tickets. I jumped at the idea as I wanted to go with her. I waited in line all day and got the tickets. I was so excited as I was going to my first ballet.

Seeing the Russian Ballet changed my life. I knew I wanted to be part of the dance world, but I did not know what that meant at the time. I had never seen such huge, unbelievably gorgeous men before. After that I would go to the San Francisco Ballet, but the men and women were all so small and skinny.

I began to ask Esther about her life in Russia. As she was a very educated woman, I was fascinated to learn how her life was so different from Annie's life in Russia. Annie had been a peasant. Esther was from the intelligentsia. I knew nothing of class consciousness until I met Esther. She explained how happy she was in the U.S. as she did not feel the pain of being a Jew she had felt in Russia.

Esther gave me her car as she no longer used it and did not want to pay the garage fees. Now I had my own car—her car! I was so happy. I felt, *she must love me*. Esther began taking a bus to the beach, but only once a week. For our other visit each week, I would go to her downtown apartment. She would serve me Russian food that was delicious and healthy.

I was beginning to want to leave my husband as I was painfully unhappy being with a man who could not express any kind of feeling. I had been friends with Esther for two years, and I now felt I needed to go on with my life. I was also miserable in my sexual frustration. Sex with Joe was a duty. I knew there had to be more out of life. Living with the mindset of a victim, just doing my duty, I had been repeating my mother's life.

Esther said to me one day, "I think you need to be with a woman." I looked at her and could not believe that such words had come out of her mouth. This was the 50s, and the idea of homosexuality was still incomprehensible to me. But I knew Esther had spoken the words I needed to hear.

A few months later, I went to the local Jewish community center to swim with two girlfriends of mine. The lifeguard was a masculine woman. She was looking at me. I felt something in her that was in me, but I could not name it. Because of my feeling, I walked over to her and asked if she thought I could get a job at the center. She said she would hire me whenever I was ready. I felt such gratitude and happiness. I could become a lifeguard at this great place where everybody was so friendly.

Esther was very pleased when I told her I had found the possibility of a job at the Jewish Center. Little did I know that I was going to meet my first actual lover at the center. I stopped seeing Esther as I worked every day. One day she came by the center and I was standing by the pool with Liz, who was to become my first woman lover. As we all stood there talking, I kept thinking that Esther had told me I should be with a woman. And now I was! Esther clearly understood. She smiled at me as she left the center.

I didn't see Esther again for 20 years. She was 70 years old when I saw her again and by that time I no longer felt attached to her, but I still said "Hi, Esther."

As she walked away, she said in a cold and arrogant manner, "Why don't you come up and see me sometime?" But my life was full by then, and I never did.

Chapter 21, Making the Impossible Possible

In June 1960, I could no longer deny my sexual attraction to women. I had to ask my husband, Joe, to leave. He was a very handsome man but shut down and emotionally unavailable. After Joe left, I needed more money than I was making at the Jewish Center to pay the mortgage and buy food. I asked my friend Lana if she would like to live with me. She was in the process of leaving her husband. She agreed to pay rent and also pay me for child care. What a disaster! Lana had two adorable children, Randy, 5, and Shirley, 4. They loved to play with my daughters who were 5 and 3. I agreed to take care of her children during the day while she worked and thought this would be a great job. To my disappointment, Lana took advantage. She stayed out late every night or brought strange men home. I was stuck in the house, day after day. After 5 months I went into a deep depression along with a cold that hung around like the San Francisco fog. I had no life of my own. There was no surfing, no walks on the beach and no social life. Joe kept saying during his weekly visits, "Don't you want me to come back home?" He recognized that I could no longer function and wanted to help. It worked to his advantage because he missed his family.

Lana and I used to be very close friends until she moved in. Her behavior radically changed when she became single. I felt abandoned by her. I lost her friendship and my freedom. The accumulation of Joe wanting to return, Lana not being available, and my illness wore me down.

One weekend, I went up to Lake Tahoe with my daughters and when I returned home, I found my house full of feces—someone had broken into my home, and had defecated all over the hallway. I had to ask Lana to leave and Joe happily returned.

The next week, it was extremely foggy as I was walking across the street when all of sudden I was hit by a car. The man who hit me was so old, he could not see me, and knew he caused the accident. I was taken to the hospital with a concussion; my face was black and blue for two weeks. The benefit of this accident, besides getting two thousand dollars, was a woman who lay in the hospital bed next to mine taught me what a marriage should look like: she communicated with her husband for an hour every day, while Joe visited me and just sat there. I knew then that I must divorce Joe, but I was still not strong enough to leave him. We even went to one session of therapy, I really wanted to try but he just could not talk about his feelings.

I returned to my great life running and swimming in the ocean. In a month, I felt strong again. One day at Aquatic Park, I ran into my friend, Ray, a trainer of long distance swimmers. He was ten years older than I was, quite handsome, with a warm personality. He had been observing me swimming in the bay and told me I should train with him for the San Francisco Golden Gate Swim in July, which was held under the Golden Gate Bridge. I said to him, "I can't swim that fast."

Ray responded, "Oh, yes, you can. I will train you for the swim. It will take about a year. After that year, you will be able to swim in any long distance swim in the world." I believed him as he had a reputation as a great coach.

I knew he had a crush on me as he was always staring at me on the beach. I began my rigorous daily training running a mile in the sand and swimming around the cove three times, which was a mile. Ray made me race faster all the time as he told me I had to develop my speed. "That is what will get you through the rough current under the bridge," he said.

In January of 1962, after training for a year, I was so strong in both body and mind from the daily discipline that I was ready to divorce Joe. I had met Jack, a lawyer, who informed me I was entitled to child support. With my finances secured, January 3rd, my birthday, became my liberation day. Jack, the lawyer and teacher, believed I would leave my husband and be with him once I was a free woman. He graciously processed my divorce for free. When the final papers were filed, he said, "Now we can finally have sex, let's go to a hotel."
I told him, "No, I can't do that. I want to be with a woman."

He said, "I can't believe I did all this for you and now you tell me you want to be with a woman!"

I wasn't sexually attracted to him and didn't want to tell him, so I kept on running with him on the beach as we had become friends. I felt that was the least I could do for all he had done for me.

The way I suffered from the divorce was with my beautiful daughter Roxanne's lament for her father. She was just 3 ½ years old and adored Joe. When he did not come home the second night, she looked up at me with those warm, loving brown eyes and asked, "Is Daddy not coming home anymore?" When I answered, "No," the look on her beautiful, sad face devastated me. I did not know what to do. Denial was the rule in the family, so I ignored my feelings.

Her relationship with her sister Despina became her salvation. They saw their father every Wednesday and Sunday. At least he was always physically there for them.

I returned to my job at the Jewish Community Center in San Francisco. I was a lifeguard and taught swimming. I taught older adults and gave them the confidence to dive and swim which they never thought they were capable of doing. Herb Cann, a writer for the San Francisco Chronicle would tell me that I was a great teacher. I began to believe this feedback and it lit a fire in my imagination of what my life would be like if I were to become a teacher.

There was nothing ordinary about these times. For me I had to leave my husband. I knew I had to seek out my life as a lesbian no matter how difficult it might be. Being in the closet no longer fit me. Even though I had two beautiful daughters, I had to somehow make it on my own. Coming out in such a homophobic time was like walking into a dark tunnel with no light on the other end. Just meeting that one lesbian at the Jewish Community Center made me realize there must be more.

Chapter 22, My First Love Affair

Three weeks after my divorce, Liz walked into my life. It was like a thunderbolt of energy had blasted into my life when she entered the pool area in a warm, white bathing suit—at least it felt warm to me. There was something very familiar about her, like she was an old friend and I wanted to reconnect. People gathered around her immediately. She was hot! I was immediately drawn to her. After she dove off the diving board with such precision, she swam up to me at the end of pool.

Sitting on my lifeguard stool I basked in her warm, loving smile. It totally captivated me as she said, "And who are you?" Our blue eyes became mesmerized with each other. Unfortunately, this was the era of not being open about your gay sexuality. She told me of her boyfriend, living in London and I knew it was a lie.

Everyone at the Jewish Community Center knew Liz. She was a famous artist and a world traveler who was talked about by many people who belonged to the center. At the time I met her, she was having an art exhibit there. There was an article about her on the bulletin board from when she had been interviewed by Herb Cain of the San Francisco Chronicle newspaper. I was honored to know her.

Liz and I loved playing with each other in the water. The men soon joined in, and we began a daily playtime together. They would put us up on their shoulders, and Liz and I would try to push each other off. Life was great fun, but a lot more than fun, I was soon to find out. For three weeks, we played and flirted. The weekends without seeing her only made me anxious for Mondays when her warm face touched my heart. The gathering electricity between us affected my ability to sleep. The intensity between us was something I had never experienced before. I felt the feelings were mutual, but we never spoke of it. One day, when she came into the Center to talk to me, she wore men's slacks. In 1960s, women didn't wear men's clothing, therefore, I came to the conclusion that she might be like me, a lesbian.

When I told Liz I had two daughters, she was excited to meet them as she didn't have children of her own. I invited her to dinner the following week, and the girls met her in their pretty dresses. It was love at first sight. They shared stories of their lives. The girls, 7 and 4, kept Liz totally enraptured. As I watched this scene unfold, I felt grateful and happy to be part of it. The four of us together were my idea of a real loving family, my heart was full of joy. What a contrast between Liz and my life with Joe who didn't talk. But here we were, laughing, sharing and creating a magical moment in time. The love spilled over.

That night I told Liz I was in love with her shyly, I could not face her. I was too afraid of rejection. She turned my head around and planted a big kiss on my lips. With that kiss, I felt I was being kissed for the first time: so soft, so sensual. She explored the texture of my lips, discovering me with such tenderness, I melted. This was such a contrast with how men kissed, hard, aggressive and penetrating my mouth with their protruding tongue. Liz's kiss implied an invitation to go further. I took her hand and we ran to my bedroom. We went to bed that night and were like two wild animals with such longing and hunger coming out of the both of us. It was beyond passion. It was like two lost souls had finally found each other.

The next morning, I wanted to discuss what had transpired between us, but Liz said she had to get back to her studio. I felt so lonely once again, and feared I was repeating a pattern established with Joe of no communication. The fog of doom lifted when Liz called me later that day to invite me and the girls to meet her mother who was confined to a wheelchair. When we met her mother, my exuberant joy lifted her out of the chair. I kissed her cheek warmly. Here was the family I wanted to have all my life. Again, it was a loving time. I forgot wanting to talk about my feelings and put my needs on the back burner, fearful to disturb the loving scene that was unfolding in front of me. I was in love. The deep love I had for Liz kept me denying my need to communicate with her. The sex was enough, or so I thought. My daughters were very happy with Liz, too, so I ignored my longing for heartfelt talks.

I was also surrounded by many loving artistic friends of Liz who embraced me with open arms. I became lost in Liz's world. My life was rich with parties, gays who never talked about being gay—just about work, art, and theater. Liz would introduce me as her "friend," never her lover. I was locked into the San Francisco homophobic world of the 60s. Everyone at that time was homophobic, even the gays.

After four wonderful months of having my lifelong dream realized and playing honeymoon, Liz informed me she had to leave for her usual time in New York. After that she was going to Europe for three months to paint. I had made Liz the center of my life, but she had a full life without me. I thought we were in love, how could she so easily up and leave? I was going to lose that love, that connection. I was still reeling with these unwelcomed news, when she said, causally, "Come with me."

I couldn't figure out how to make that happen. How could I be with her? I had two children, a house, a job, and no money. Then, as if on cue, I met a man on the beach who was a realtor. He informed me that my home would sell easily. Within a week, the house was sold and I found an apartment close to where Liz lived, even though she had already left for New York. I saw her mother daily and that somehow made me feel close to Liz while I got my finances in order for my planned trip to New York. Liz had encouraged me to register for college. I missed Liz so much. I registered at San Francisco City College for the fall semester, as I had decided to take everyone's encouragement to be a teacher. Especially Liz's.

Chapter 23, The Golden Gate Swim and Europe

I made the decision to cancel the swim competition for which I had been training the preceding year. It was scheduled for July and by that time I planned to be in Europe with Liz. When I told Ray, my coach, I was not going to be able to swim in July, he was disappointed and angry. He had been counting on me to make the swim—I was his prize student. He didn't speak to me for a few weeks. Then, he came up to me one day at Aquatic Park and said, "What I want to do with you is totally illegal, but I *need* to see you make that Golden Gate swim. You must promise you will never tell anyone. We are going to do the swim at dawn, by ourselves. Just to prove to you, you can do it."

The early morning of the swim, May 15, 1962, was extremely foggy, which was good because no one could see us. Ray greased me down heavily so I would be able to take the freezing cold water that flows under the Golden Gate bridge. The fog horn blasted, I was so nervous, but somewhere deep inside of me I knew I had to make this swim. I jumped into the dark freezing water with Ray next to me in his big boat yelling instructions at me. I could barely hear him because of the noise of the fog horns blasting. Ray had a big gun to kill the sharks if they got too near. I swam like I had never swum before. The current was so powerful in the middle of the bridge that I had to kick faster and faster to get through it as Ray kept yelling, "You can do it! You can do it!" All I could see was dark water as I got my second wind. I was in an altered state and felt like I was flying through the water, and I could go on for hours. I had never felt so powerful as I swam through that horrific current.

The swim lasted 25 minutes, as it was only a half mile. When I reached the other side, I could not believe I had actually finished. Fear and the determination that I could do it had been my motivation. The months of training had worked. I felt overwhelmed with joy and grateful that Ray had had such confidence and faith in me. Accomplishing the swim gave me the confidence that maybe I could make it through college, even though academics never interested me.

Around that same time, I found myself arranging to leave my girls with their father's family. I had no qualms about the arrangement. Joe and his entire Greek family doted upon the girls. They would be surrounded by love from all angles. My dreams were finally happening, going to New York with my lover and being able to travel, as had been my lifelong dream. I thought traveling with Joe to

Kentucky would soothe my travel lust, but it didn't. It only stimulated me for more adventures. I bought a round trip ticket to New York for $99, and left on June 1st with the intention of spending three months in Europe with Liz.

The rickety old plane was left over from World War II. I could see the pilot and the engine from my seat and I worried if it was bolted to the floorboards. The plane bounced the entire six hours cross country to New York. When I arrived at La Guardia Airport, the look on Liz's face frightened me. This was not the look of love, but rather disappointment. It was an unfamiliar look that I had not seen before. I had been filled with excitement and my heart dropped to my stomach because she was not excited to see me. I questioned if I had misinterpreted her feeling towards me, or if I had made a horrible mistake. I was out of my league and 3,000 miles away from home.

"Why did you schlep these two big suitcases? I told you to travel light!" she said with anger in her voice.

"You didn't explain to me what you meant by 'travel light.' I had no idea what that meant," I said in my defense.

Liz immediately took me to buy a rucksack in silence. We would be doing a lot of hitchhiking in Europe and traveling to different countries, therefore mobility was important. But I had no clue, until I arrived at the airport and saw her face. After getting the rucksack, she finally began to talk to me, and I began to feel safe once again. I hadn't mistaken her feelings towards me after all. We made a quick stop at Goodwill and deposited all my extra clothing and suitcases. They were indeed extra baggage.

Our first night together was in a ratty, beat up hotel; we did not make love. She claimed she was exhausted. We got into bed, she went to her side and she rolled over with her back towards me. I felt ugly, not loved and again wondered what I was doing with a woman who felt like a stranger. There was no cuddling, snuggling or touching, not even a kiss. Sleep was elusive as I questioned why I was there, again. I felt horrible and horny as hell as we had not been together for a month. I awoke at dawn and ran up the street to the Empire State Building. I had so much pent up sexual energy that I easily climbed the 102 floors to the observation deck, thanks to my vigorous training for the Golden Gate swim. At least physical exertion was my way to manage those out of control sexual desires. That had always worked for me, and I didn't need Liz to take care of my needs. I was able to syphon off some of that excess energy through my climb. As I exited the building, there was Liz, with a frightened look on her face. Part of me was glad to see she *did* have feelings for me. We went to breakfast and only discussed the plans we had for the day. This was the way she would relate to me. There was no talk about the previous night or about feelings. I had again, chosen an emotionally unavailable person.

Liz would travel with her watercolor materials and paint the many sights in the city while I visited museums, galleries and walked the streets. Upon my return she would ask me all kinds of questions, which was great. Unfortunately, just like Joe, Liz would not talk about her feelings. She was also as unavailable as my mother. I noticed a pattern that still exists to this day, picking emotionally unavailable women. I adored Liz because she was so interesting, fun-loving and I didn't know better at the time.

Liz had always traveled alone until this trip. She had friends all over the world. I was happy to be with her, but uncomfortable when feelings came up and I couldn't talk about them. I had to stuff them. On the other hand, it was exciting being with her. She had been an actress in New York so she knew many people. David Wood, a friend of Liz who danced with the Martha Graham dance company, let me attend a class with Martha. In that lesson, I learned a great deal about dance contractions, which she was famous for.

We attended a party at the home of Pat Covici, who was a publisher of Saul Bellow and Arthur Miller at Viking Press. Saul Bellow took a liking to me, but I found him too full of himself to want to spend time with him. Liz was always showing her paintings as people loved to buy them, and that was how she made her way in the world. When Arthur Miller walked into the room with Marilyn Monroe at his side I was impressed. Marilyn was very shy and withdrawn as Arthur took center stage.

Ten days later, we left for London. The entire day, upon our arrival, I walked around with my mouth open. It was so big, impressive, and foreign! I knew nothing of world history so I had a lot to learn on this trip.

Liz's friends were all in theatre and quite friendly. Liz's ex-lover, Melanie, a warm loving lesbian, wanted us all to sleep together, but I was not in for that. I was introduced to David and Marcie, Liz's friends, who were married unhappily because David was gay. He needed Marcie as a cover up, which Marcie hated. She told me how hard it was to be married to a gay man whom she adored, but who could not make love to her. This was the beginning of learning how homophobic Europe was at that time.

After London, we went to Paris. I became seasick crossing the English Channel but was surprised when Liz took such good care of me. She mothered me, with care and concern. I felt her love, and it made up for all the hiding of our feelings. I recovered quickly in Paris, the city of love. I was taken with seeing so many people kiss openly. That would also be true in Italy. These were only straight people, of course.

I loved the Impressionist painters. Van Gogh was my favorite, as I could feel his suffering. I could see why he was one of the most famous painters in the world and he died so young at 32.

The Louvre Museum and the streets of Paris were a delight to walk in with their many shops, cafes, and interesting people. We stayed in a lovely, little old hotel on the left bank of the Seine River that had a stand up toilet, which felt more comfortable than a sit-down toilet. By this time, though, I began to miss my daughters terribly, and Liz could not deal with my pain. I felt so alone with her when she would say, "Write a card to them." To my (mis)fortune, the wine was cheap and delicious. I loved how it numbed my feelings. I used alcohol to cope with pain and any type of stress. I would use it to lower my inhibitions, to act out and just be myself.

After a week in Paris, we hitchhiked to Venice, Italy. This has to be the most majestic city in the world. With its many canals of water, we had to walk or take a boat. We stayed in a big youth hostel on one of the many canals. I wanted to jump into the water so badly, I missed my daily swims that would quiet my nervous energy. We met many very interesting people from all over the world, which made it a wonderful experience. The hostel and one meal per day cost two dollars.

By the time we arrived in Florence, I saw that Italian men were the biggest flirts in the world. Many young men were looking for foreign woman to take care of them. They thought nothing of coming up and kissing total strangers, as it happened to me many times. We stayed in a hostel in Florence, which was a huge palace of the former mistress of Mussolini. Liz was always painting, so I went to many museums by myself and loved it. Michelangelo's David amazed me. I had never seen such a huge statue so beautifully created.

Rome was grand with its bridges, mansions, and huge parks that I could walk in all day. The highlight for me was the Sistine Chapel. I loved lying on the floor and looking up at Michelangelo's ceiling. It was obvious that he loved the human body, especially men.

After our time in Italy, Liz and I took a boat across the Mediterranean to Greece. The color of the sea was memorable, so distinctly blue and green. The way the sunlight danced on the water made it look like glittering diamonds. I've had Greeks as close family of choice for many years. First there was my neighbor Hercules and his family. I married into the Greek culture with Joe as my husband. Their warmth, music, and food was such a contrast with my cold, distant family. When I arrived in Greece, everything felt like the home of my heart. Greek dancing every night was fun and familiar. Needless to say, it was effortless to indulge in the lusciously flavored Greek food that I had missed since I separated from Joe.

Three weeks later, we headed back up north to the Netherlands on a train that was *fabuloso*: people were so friendly, sharing food and conversation. Sweden had the most gorgeous women cleaning the streets in Stockholm. We stayed in a large ship that had been turned into a youth hostel. Norway was one of the most sociable and friendly of the northern countries. Strangers would offer help and be curious about our travels. They warmly offered suggestions about what we should see and places that only the locals knew about. Because we stayed in youth hostels most of the time, we met many people from all over the world. About twice a week when Liz and I wanted to be intimate, we stayed in historical places converted into hotels for five dollars a night. I had gone from slumming it in hostels, to a palace. Although we never talked about feelings, those nights we were intimate satiated my physical needs, but not my emotional ones. She told me she loved me, but I never felt it. I would see how loving she was with strangers, but never me. I was replaying that old familiar pattern; first my unavailable mother, then Joe, now Liz. At the time, the way I dealt with my feelings was to numb them with alcohol. That worked for a while.

Our summer vacation came to an end. On the plane, I sat next to a very interesting man who had studied all summer at a university in Germany. He encouraged me to tell him about my trip because his head was stuck in books, while mine was taking in different cultures and countries. For the next tearful five hours crossing the Atlantic, I shared my impression of the uniqueness of all the countries I travelled through. Each country had its own individual language, food, money, and history. My tears were a mixture of sadness because the trip had concluded, and my heart spilled over in gratitude for having had the adventure of a lifetime. For $500, I had the most incredible time of my life!

After three months, I couldn't wait to see my girls. I wanted to go home, get my daughters, and return to Europe with them. In years to come we were to do this many times. After I returned to San Francisco, when I climbed the hill to the house where my girls were staying, my passionate Despina came running down the hill into my arms. Our bliss mixed together with tears streaming from our eyes. We were both filled with joy and relief in being together. Another memorable moment, a perfect ending to my adventure.

Chapter 24, San Francisco City Junior College

I was so excited to begin my studies after my trip to Europe, which had opened my mind to a world filled with questions. I climbed the hill to San Francisco City College observing the engraving on top of the main building that proclaimed, "The truth shall make you free." Thanks to my wonderful trip to Europe, I knew *my truth:* I wanted to be a history teacher. To be a teacher I had to take subjects many of which I had no interest in. I could see that my karma had caught up with me from all the cheating I had done previously in school. I felt like a first grader when it came to writing a paper. Thanks to Liz who had been an English major at UC Berkeley, I was able to write pretty decent ones. She was a great teacher.

I loved English classes because of the literature. Psychology classes also fascinated me and encouraged further learning about the human psyche. Most science, such as physics, chemistry, and anatomy did not interest me, but geology did. My fascination with the earth science helped me learn about earthquakes, especially having lived through the San Francisco earthquake of 1957 when my fireplace caved in.

The guidance counselors at the school had told me that there were no jobs for history teachers, but women were needed to teach physical education. Because I was a natural athlete, the choice was easy. I made the switch thinking I would still be free to travel for three months. I kept history and psychology as minors, but majored in physical education.

If it had not been for all my physical education and humanities classes, I would not have gotten into San Francisco State. I loved the P.E. classes, and I got A's in all of them. That averaged out the C's I got in my science and other classes. Even so, I would never have made it through school if it had not been for Liz helping me correct my writing assignments.

Joe would take the girls every Sunday and Wednesday so I could study all day. Friday night was movie night with the girls and Liz. We would pack up hamburgers and go to see all the black and white Warner Brothers films. These movies were shown at a special old theater on Market Street where we only paid fifty cents for adults and twenty-five cents for children.

Joe said to me one day, "You will never make it through college." Instead of discouraging me, it made me determined that I would show him I could. Joe was the opposite. He had dropped out of college to drive a truck delivering bread. He liked life to be easy. I don't think he challenged his fears. He had suffered too much losing his mother and his father being unavailable to be able to take on more hardship.

I was determined to show Joe I could do it; but I was still scared of failing. Liz's mother, Grandma Lipschultz, really helped me with my fears as she constantly encouraged me. I was the first one in my own family who was to finish college. I was not able to get any encouragement from anyone in my family, no surprise there. I also found Yoga at this time to quiet my nerves, and it helped me study and absorb more of what I read as I had a hard time focusing.

Fear did not just revolve around school; it had become my agenda. I felt so bad I was not there for my daughters. I neglected them emotionally, just as my mother had done with me. My all-consuming fear about not graduating left me totally preoccupied. Thank goodness for Liz. She was their emotional anchor, however, she and I didn't communicate either verbally or sexually. She was too busy in her professional life to devote the time the relationship needed to grow. Recognizing my libido was more pronounced than hers, I began to take advantage of all the male attention coming my way. I began having affairs with men while Liz was away on business trips. This was my secret and hidden from Liz. Part of me rationalized that it was acceptable because my father provided the role model.

Liz and I stayed together for 7 years. Her goal was to see me established in my teaching career and therefore able to take care of myself and the girls. Even though I eventually told her about the affairs in our 6th year, she remained an additional year. There was no sex between us, she had a sense of obligation and remained in the relationship but pulled further and further away emotionally.

I shall never forget that memorable Saturday, it was a horrible painful moment. It was a cold winter day in our 7th year, she came to my house. In her hand was a large lithograph depicting a hand-drawn picture of us kissing. We loved kissing. Liz and Stan were the only two people who I loved kissing. She presented it to me along with the words, "I can no longer be with you and the girls. You're bi-sexual and I'm not. I'm not going to see you anymore."

I stood there, mouth open, in shock. Why would she want to leave? It was the 70s and free love was as common as a handshake, especially in San Francisco. I tried over the years to make contact for the girls' sake, but deep down, I know it was mostly for my own. I wrote letters, called, and received no response. I have continued to want contact her for the last 44 years. Even though at the time of this writing she was 92 years old and wheelchair bound, she refused to see me. I have been paying for my promiscuity for the last 45 years—interestingly enough my father got away with that type of behavior all his life.

Mom with George, Dottie (left) and me (right)

Dottie (left) and me (right), George in the buggy

Grandpa O'Connor with me and Dottie

Dottie (right) and me (left)

Graduation from St. Brendan's Grammar School

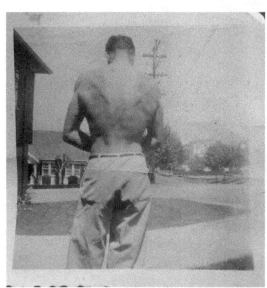

Joe

Ray, my swim coach, and me at Golden Gate Bridge

Joe, Despina, and me

Despina and me

OCT 1958

Joe and Roxanne

Roxanne and Despina

My daughters and me

Chapter 25, San Francisco State College

I didn't pass the English placement exam which left me taking the remedial class. When I entered the class, I easily had ten years on the rest of the students. The teacher was this gorgeous, big African American man. He smiled at me as I was 26, the oldest student in the class. The others were teenagers, so he was happy to meet an adult. There was an instant attraction between us, but I ignored it. *He was my teacher, after all!*

After we wrote our first paper in class he asked me to stay. I was scared because this was the first paper I had written without Liz's proofreading. But underlining our encounter was a current of sexual attraction that went against my prejudices. I was fighting this strong desire, with my first venture into crossing the race barrier. I imagined him telling me that I could not even be in his class. When he asked me, "Why are you in this class? You write very well." I told him I froze whenever I had to write under pressure. I had no confidence. He said, "Ok, we shall deal with that." I got As on all my papers because I loved the subjects he assigned us to write in class. This was a tumultuous time to be alive. There were student protests in Berkeley and the anti-Vietnam war movement was at its peak. I was politically educated by going to all the demonstrations and listening to people like Mario Savio and Joan Baez.

At the end of the semester, he suggested I visit him at his home before the final exam. I obeyed him and I trusted his judgment, besides, he was very attractive. My curiosity was piqued. The exam was to be at 1 p.m. I arrived at his home at 10 a.m., as he requested. He took me upstairs to his bedroom and asked me to take my clothes off. I asked, "Why?"

He said, "I want to make love to you for 2 hours so you will be relaxed for your exam, and you will pass." I had total confidence with his suggestion, besides according to my father, sex was all I was good for as he had repeated throughout my 18 years under his roof. I had been impressed with this teacher's knowledge and wisdom. I was putty in his hands, so I did what he said. Besides, he was a hunk!

This was not an act of love. He was determined to prove to me, that when I was relaxed, I could write. After two hours of sexual gymnastics, I went back to school to face the exam without fear. I passed with such ease, surprised at how relaxed I was. He had sat in the room and watched me for the entire hour of the test and after it was over he said, "Goodbye." His intention proved to me I could pass an exam under pressure. It worked! I saw him a year later, and he just smiled at me. I wondered if he did that to all his older students. I never asked.

When I entered San Francisco State, I was excited to find out that I could have an emphasis in dance instead of sports for the Physical Education Major. I really loved dance and wanted to learn more about how to teach it. During my 3 years at SF State I took all the dance classes offered, even special workshops that were held on weekends. I received Cs in my History and other academic classes, which were harder than those at City College, but I had all As in my dance classes. This averaged to a B, which I needed for my GPA.

Joan Baez and her husband came to the college for demonstrations against the Vietnam War, and I would take my daughters, who were 12 and 15, to these events. I wanted them to be exposed to these thoughts and ideas, to fill their young minds with history unfolding in front of their eyes. The hippy, black, and every kind of revolution went on in this school. These were extensions of the protests at Berkeley. The Black Panthers in their black leather jackets, pants, and boots closed the school down for protests to show students we needed to become aware of the racism in our country. There was only one black teacher in the school, and he was my English teacher and my one-time 2 hour sexual marathon partner.

I got a better education politically at San Francisco State than I would have at any other school because of the societal upheaval of the times. Every day somebody spoke out against the injustices in our society. Values were up for questioning and I was part of it. These new thoughts and ideas changed my way of thinking and being. These were electric times; each day was a new adventure with unpredictable events unfolding around me. My education came from living in those times, from participating, from listening to speakers, but not from books. San Francisco State was featured on many news channels and friends from across the country would comment on how fortunate I was to experience history in the making. My daughters became aware of what was going on and they too were affected by the events at that time along with the rest of our generation.

Younger gay women in my classes talked openly about their relationships, how they felt and how difficult it was being in the closet. After being in a closeted relationship with Liz for 8 years I finally found my voice and was heard and listened to by others, maybe for the first time in my life. Goodness knows my husband didn't listen, nor my mother, nor anyone else in my family. I was appreciated for being "seen and not heard." But now I had a voice, and pride in authentically being my true self.

This coming home to myself started in the P.E. department with a lesbian teacher. All the lesbian students had a crush on her including me. We would be encouraged to talk openly about our feelings and about our sexual choices. I felt relieved being around other lesbians who were proud to be gay. I wasn't "weird" especially after all the clandestine gay experiences in my past. I was sneaking around and hiding, but not at San Francisco State University. This was several years before Gay Liberation, but I felt liberated, identifying with being "Gay." The teacher who was an openly gay woman talked about her own relationship. She encouraged and supported us to be true to ourselves. Our teacher would take moments to talk to us personally, inquiring how we were doing and if there was any way she could help. Not only did I find my voice, but I also had the support I never counted on in my life.

A new world opened up for me. I could speak, I could be myself, I could be openly gay. This marked the true beginning of my adult life.

I had an astute dance teacher who warned me, "You are going to have a hard time teaching in the physical education department in the San Francisco high schools." I never knew what she meant until I began teaching dance. Then I realized it was because most of the gym teachers were "bull dykes," women whose essence is more masculine, and I was not. I did not fit into their closeted form of being gay. I was openly gay, and they were not. This was a repeat of my previous experiences with the life I was living with Liz. She was in the closet and so were her friends. We never talked about our relationships and in a sense lived in denial, both with ourselves and the outside world.

My beatnik background in the 60s influenced me more than the Hippy generation. I remembered seeing Allen Ginsberg in the Spaghetti Factory restaurant in North Beach reading his poetry and loving his outrageous spin on the hypocrisy of the government and our society. Hearing my neighbor Janis Joplin sing were memorable moments—nobody could wail and sing like Janis. The anti-material establishment I was fighting against came out when I first heard Alan Watts who first captured my attention to rebelling against my catholic background. His eastern humanistic philosophy brought out a new interest that fascinated me. However, I would go on with my spiritual search until encountering my Buddhist practice.

Chapter 26, George Washington High School: 1967-1972

My good fortune occurred when I was hired for my first job teaching at George Washington High School. Its reputation preceded it as one of the best schools in San Francisco. I felt extremely grateful and was on cloud nine for two weeks especially after having been chosen out of thirty other women for the position. I was assigned three classes of physical education and two classes of U.S. History. I loved my new boss, the principal, Ms. Albright. She was an elegant woman, and I knew she was a lesbian. We hit it off right away. Mr. Kenny, the History department head, was a kind man, always smiling and encouraging me. He mentored me in my first year.

The reason this school hired me was due to my age and my single parent status. I was eager and excited but when I arrived on my first day, things changed drastically. I had a new boss in the P.E. department. Ms. Smith, the new department head, greeted me with a forced smile. I felt a painful tension between us immediately. She put me through hell for the next 7 years. She would *ignore* my suggestions for change, *ignore* my input in department meetings, and arrive unannounced in my class and walk through, *ignoring* any order I had achieved with the students. All this *"ignoring"* triggered those old feelings again, just when I thought they had been resolved. I knew she was in the closet while I was open about my sexuality and that may have played a part in her behavior towards me. She did like my lover Liz, buying her paintings and wanting to have private conversations with her.

I loved Mr. Kenny. He was always so encouraging and balanced out Ms. Smith's open dislike for me. In spite of that, I enjoyed teaching P.E. Thank goodness I loved my students who always stimulated me to be a better teacher.

Teaching history was a challenge because most of the students were not interested in U.S. history. Mr. Kenny helped me with new ideas, and my goal every day was to make the class interesting. I used guest speakers and historical films and constantly asked the students questions to spur their curiosity.

The war in Vietnam was going on at this time. I tried to teach the students about cause and effect to help them understand why wars are created. When we studied the Russian Revolution, I assigned half the class the roles of Mensheviks, which were the affluent intelligentsia. The other half became Bolsheviks, the poor people. They really got into studying, and we had a revolution in the class with each side being able to take a stand. Of course they made so much noise, I was asked not to have any more demonstrations in my history classes.

My first years of teaching concurred with daily protests in Berkeley and San Francisco concerning the war in Vietnam and the civil rights movement. When Martin Luther King was killed on April 11, 1968, the black students united. There was a mural in the school hallway which showed a black slave being beaten by white people. One day the black students organized a demonstration and walked out of class in protest of the abuse shown on the mural. This was an amazing feat for the African American students. The slave was removed from the mural by a black artist. I found him to be a brilliant man and asked if I could have him help me teach African American history. I had not learned about Black history in any of my studies and saw this young man to be the teacher I could learn from given his personal experience and knowledge. He agreed to volunteer his time and energy to help educate the students, and myself. The students were active participants, listened, asked questions, and engaged the entire hour. Quite the change from their usual apathy. I, also, learned a great deal from him. After this experience, a black woman was hired to teach Black history for the first time ever at the school.

My students would come back after lunch stoned. They would nod off or fall asleep in the middle of class so I felt I needed to stimulate them in a new way. I suggested to my principal that we introduce psychology into the school curriculum. And she agreed. Since I had minored in psychology, I felt I could teach it and was happy when it replaced my history assignments. To my amazement, the new classes became therapeutic sessions, and I was able to connect with my students on a more personal level than before. This was my greatest victory as a teacher. I had succeeded in stimulating their curiosity about how their minds worked and how their environments affected them. They were being listened to without judgment and stopped coming to class stoned. We also talked about the returning veterans from Vietnam and their issues, now identified as Post Traumatic Stress Disorder. They paid attention, stayed awake, and hopefully developed compassion for each other. Today, psychology classes are still in the curriculum in most of the high schools in San Francisco.

One semester I had a brilliant, straight A student in one of my psychology classes, Peter. He refused to read any of the books on my class syllabus. He would only write about Nichiren Daishonin, a 13th century Japanese radical monk. Since he was not on the reading list, I gave Peter a B in the course. He did not care. I did not understand Peter until I went to my first Buddhist meeting two years later in 1971. Then I heard about Nichiren and his humanistic teachings, and decided to become a Buddhist. Peter was thrilled. He told me it was worth his receiving a B in my class.

I had promised my daughters I would take them to Europe after my first year of teaching. I saved half of my salary every month for this amazing adventure. Liz and I were not on very good terms as our relationship was going through a difficult time. Actual proof of this was that we went to the Oakland Airport instead of the San Francisco airport where our flight was to depart from. We had a chartered flight which meant there was no changing flights.

I was in such a panic, my brother threw our bags in the back of his truck and we raced over the Bay Bridge to the San Francisco airport frightened and chanting Nam Myoho Renge Kyo. When I ran up to the check-in desk the lady said she was sorry but we had missed our flight.

"No we have to be on that flight, I must talk to someone!" I reproached. They let me talk to the pilot and he brought the plane back on the runway; thank goodness the flight had been delayed. When we got on the plane every one stood up and clapped for us. I was in a shocked dazed the entire flight to London. I could not believe what had happened.

When we arrived in London, Liz was angry and that became a most painful 3 months. Despina was bored and Roxanne and Liz were their usual closed selves. I knew my relationship with Liz was ending and I was in pain the entire trip. Liz had said she wanted to see me have a career and that she did. I loved teaching.

Chapter 27, Julius Friedman

Dottie arranged a blind date for me. When Julius Friedman appeared at my door, I was immediately drawn to his humor and warmth. He entered my life laughing. "You left your keys in your door," he said as he dangled them in front of me. I was impressed with his self confidence; it immediately broke the uncomfortable tension of being "set-up." Julius was a big man, former newspaper writer, and a smart salesman just like my father. We went out, and he asked me questions about my life all evening. I was impressed to have a man interested in me and my daughters.

I had felt so alone because Liz was away traveling and Dottie kept on saying I needed the strength of a man. Being Jewish, he was impressed that I loved Israel. I had so many Jewish friends who had greatly influenced my life, including Liz. How could I not love Israel?

Julius and I dated for a while, and I was surprised he never asked me to stay with him. We were not lovers but were friends, and that felt okay, at least at the beginning. When he finally asked me to sleep with him, it was a disaster. He was impotent. I was terribly frustrated.

Months later, I found out that a fight or an argument turned him on. When I met his mother, I realized where this disturbance might have begun. He was always having desperate communication problems with his mother on the phone or when we went to visit her. They had a horrible push-pull relationship, and she was always crying about something she believed to be his fault. He was the only child and felt responsible for her.

When Julius and I would fight, he would become sexually aroused. He gave me my first orgasm and that had me hooked. I was 35 years old. I felt very dependent on him, and I learned a great deal from this very intelligent man. Since he had been secretary of the Democratic party in California, he was able to take me to interesting gatherings where I met many important political figures like Pierre Salinger, President Kennedy's press Secretary of State. I became acquainted with Dianne Feinstein, who always liked to dance with me.

Julius loved my daughters, and I thought he had a healthy relationship with them. My girls were totally out of control in the drug world. They turned to prostitution to buy heroin. I thought they would change if I were with a man, just like Dottie kept telling me. I was desperate. I didn't know what to do with my daughters, and Julius wanted to help me. Years later, I discovered that he was a sexual predator, but I was blind to any signs of this behavior due to denial of my own abuse. He discovered my daughters had been into prostitution to get drugs so he took advantage of them. I was told by Despina, years later that he had sex with my daughter Roxanne. I blame myself for bringing him into my life and my addiction to sex. These were the consequences of my denial.

At the time, out of my desperation to get my daughters out of the drug world in San Francisco, we moved to Julius's big home in San Rafael. I thought the geographic move would solve the problem, which was a total mistake. There were just as many drugs in Marin as in San Francisco. I was so naive about the drug world.

My daughters loved young African American men, and I thought that they would begin to date white boys in San Rafael. Three black girls in San Francisco were threatening to kill Despina for dating a black boy and I was scared. Despina found the only African American in Marin, but nobody threatened to kill her.

In the meantime, I was having a horrible experience with Julius. He was still very much involved with his ex-girlfriend and explained our presence in his house by saying he was helping me with my daughters. It was a fiasco from day one of our living together. My desperation in dealing with my daughters' drug addictions was so painful after a year with Julius that I moved back to San Francisco even though we kept seeing each other.

Since Julius had given me my first orgasm, I finally felt like a true woman introduced into womanhood. So this is what sex was all about! I never understood sex before, and the orgasms may have tied me to him in a way I hadn't experienced before. I don't know if it was love, because my father had told me my value was my sexuality.

He was a real estate agent specializing in selling land, and he encouraged me to find clients for him. Many of my fellow teachers bought land from him, and I did, too. Shortly after that, the company folded, and all the promises of a new community to be built on the land became non-existent. The other teachers were all mad at me, as we all had a lot of money invested and I felt I needed to leave Washington High School.

I was juggling two relationships. While Liz was traveling, I was having sex with Julius without her knowledge. My relationship with Liz changed and we became more platonic. She was ashamed of being identified as being a lesbian. One day, I went to her house. She said, "I don't want to see you anymore."

I asked, "Why?"

"You're involved with a creep. How could you be involved with such a man like that and have your daughters around him?"

She refused to see me after that day. I had chosen sex over my relationship with Liz and I lost her forever. She opened an entire world of education, schooling, travel, and culture to me. Without her, there has been a void that I attempted to fill with many different women. It has never worked. Liz was emotionally unavailable. The next day, she brought the etching of two women kissing that was the symbol of our relationship. But I never knew how she felt because there were no words spoken. Not having Liz in my life has been a devastating reality that I must live with.

In 1972, I came out of the closet with thousands of other gay people and marched down Market Street in our first gay day parade with Harvey Milk leading the way. It was one of the happiest days of my life. I had a community of gay people and I was delighted. Maud's Bar became my Friday night hangout where us lesbians could openly dance and party with each other.

Chapter 28, My Adventure with Jerry Brown, 1970

Jerry Brown and I began our relationship back in 1947 at St. Brendan's Catholic School in San Francisco. We were the first graduating class in 8th grade, and we were supposed to set an example for all the other students in the school.

The Dominican nuns were known to be strict educators and firm disciplinarians. Jerry and I became fast friends because we were always getting into trouble. We had to stay after school a lot, and that is where Jerry and I started our friendship. We sat together in the principle's office for an hour each time we got into trouble. The principal walked in and out, so we had plenty of time alone together. We loved to joke with each other. Jerry had no friends except me in the school. My friend, Happy, lived behind Jerry and she said Jerry was always a loner.

After graduation, we went our separate ways, and it was not until 1970 at a class reunion that I saw Jerry once again. He was there because he was running for Secretary of State, and he wanted us all to vote for him. Jerry and I struck up a fun conversation, and he asked me if he could see me. So we began seeing each other as friends and lovers. We enjoyed each other's company, but sex didn't work between us. We loved going to the beach together and walking in the sand along the San Francisco coastline where we laughed about so many things that struck us funny. We still were able to talk on the phone. We needed someone to talk with, and I certainly needed to talk about my daughters who were both lost in the drug world. Jerry had gone into the Jesuit priesthood after high school so I thought he could help me. That never happened.

Jerry is a brilliant, calculating man who knows what he wants and goes after it. A true Aries, he rams into everything. When he was Secretary of State, he told me he was going to be the next governor.

I said, "How can you say that?"

"My father was governor, why shouldn't I be?" was his response.

After he did become governor in 1974, I saw him only occasionally. In that first governorship, he was much more a man of the people than he became in his later terms. He used to drive a beat-up old Dodge as he would say "I don't want to waste the taxpayers' money." He also refused to live in the governor's mansion and instead, he lived in a poor neighborhood in Sacramento and slept on a mattress on the floor.

I was happy when he married his secretary a few years back. She adored him, and he certainly needed to be adored. I knew he never had that adoration as a child because his parents were too busy with their careers to have time for him.

Jerry Brown is a fine governor though he is now more traditional and understands the urgent need to focus on budget issues. I have not liked his policy of wanting to limit the student population of City College of San Francisco to youth between the ages of 18 and 21. Certainly, my experience with him and the societal turmoil and activism I witnessed when I was a student at San Francisco State University opened my awareness to political issues and how they affect the people.

Jerry was elected for his fourth term as governor. This was a first for California, and so he leaves his unique mark on the state, and in my memory.

Chapter 29, General Avraham Yoffe

General Avraham Yoffe was one of the founders of modern Israel. He was, without a doubt, the most interesting, lovable human being I have ever met. Julius, my boyfriend, introduced us after, and we were drawn to each other immediately. Julius adored Avraham, and he had no problem with my being with Avraham on the side. We were completely open about it.

My attraction to Avraham became obvious when we all took a trip to Washington State to visit the National Rainforest. In the rain he picked me up, turned me sideways in his arms, and put me up over his head. I could feel his great strength, and I felt he had taken me into his heart, as he certainly had. We became inseparable for the week that he was visiting San Francisco selling bonds to Americans for Israel's survival. I fell in love with his warmth and concern for my life. I knew I could never have a life with him, but we had an intense affair for many years. He always wrote letters to me through his secretary as he could not write in English. We had a deep connection, but I knew he belonged to Israel.

In addition to collecting money for Israel, he set about to find animals for the biblical garden he had built there. He looked all over the world for animals that existed in the time of Jesus, and I traveled with him in the deserts of the United States looking for his rare creatures. I was so much in love with him that women became only an afterthought.

When I went to Israel to visit him for the first time, his face was broadcasted on the TVs at the airport. He was talking about his biblical gardens. Avraham was well-known and influential as he had an important position in the government as Director of Nature Reserves. Since everyone knew him and he was married, we could not embrace when we met in public. He took me immediately to the Knesset, which is the house of the government. He was so happy to see me that we made love on the white marble floor. What passion, what fame, and I was the recipient.

Later, I knew I was pregnant with his son, the sensation of pregnancy differed so much from the experience I had carrying my first two baby girls. I realized I couldn't raise this child alone in addition to my daughters. I had an abortion at Kaiser thanks to Roe vs Wade. It was a very difficult decision for me as I felt I was carrying a boy and I had always wanted a boy. When I told Avraham I had aborted our child, he became very angry and asked me why. I said I was not going to raise his child alone. He told me he would have taken care of me in Israel, but as tears came down my cheeks I softly told him I was not going to live in Israel as his mistress. After that, I sat in silence while he did his work.

He took me to the Red Sea, which was one of the most beautiful places I had ever seen. The fish were unbelievable colors—rich blue, yellow, red, and orange—and we swam with them in the heat of the desert. This area was not open to the public, but Avraham was the director of the Nature Reserve so we could go anywhere. At night we made love on the plains of that desert. Suddenly, a platoon of men surprised us by parachuting down from their helicopters. They laughed as they surrounded our naked bodies. He ordered them to leave. Later he left me at my hotel, and I cried myself to sleep. I was his mistress and wanted to be so much more.

The next day Avraham took me to visit the kibbutz he had founded in the Galilee region. His son was the director there, and we visited him in his home. I was shocked to see a picture of his first wife. She looked exactly like me. After we left, I asked Avraham about her. He said, in a matter of fact manner, "She was killed by a bomb while she was riding a motorcycle." There was no emotion in his face. I knew Avraham had faced horrible atrocities that I could never even imagine.

After we visited the kibbutz, Avraham took me to visit his Arab friends in their tents. We sat on beautiful rugs with white and cobalt blue patterns while they served us delicious, rich Arab food—curried lamb, couscous, and dates. Avraham loved these people as they had grown up together. I could see the pain in his eyes when we left. He had been forced to side with his country's politics, which separated Israel from the Arabs.

Avraham was such a tender man. I heard a story about him that touched me deeply. When he was leading his troops in their tanks on the Sinai desert in the war against Egypt, he stopped them so that a baby deer could cross the road. Animals were his dearest love. All the love I saw in him emerged when he would pick up one his many animals in the Nature Reserve.

Avraham was a quiet man but he always wanted to know about my daughters. I had to keep repeating the same story as they continued to use drugs. He suggested that they come to Israel and live on his kibbutz. This gave me great hope for them, and I sent them to Israel. Unfortunately, it didn't help. My cleaver daughters found Arabs to supply them with opium.

When I went to pick them up a year later, I no longer wanted to have sex with Avraham. Barbara, my lover at the time, was with me on this trip. Avraham asked me if she and I were lovers, I told him that we were. Even so, he asked me to stay with him. I told him, "No." I always felt Avraham had women all over the world, so he could easily say to me, "That's okay." I knew he loved me, but I was one of many.

This relationship ran its course over a ten year period. In 1982, one year before he died, he came to visit me in San Francisco. He had called on the telephone begging to see me, and I agreed. On a rainy afternoon, he walked into my house, immediately took me to the floor, and made passionate love to me. Afterwards, I could feel there was something wrong with him. He was breathing heavily, and I put him in my bed. Lying there, he told me he had a horrible disease, which he could not get control of. Later, I learned that he had cancer. He said he had wanted to see me before he died. I felt sad but not devastated. There were long intervals between the times I saw him, sometimes two years would pass before we would meet. Other relationships came and went from my life. I was no longer in love with him as he was part of my painful past.

Chapter 30, Finding Nam Myoho Renge Kyo

My greatest benefit during this tumultuous time of my life was finding my Buddhist practice, which I have been doing now for 45 years. I was first introduced to chanting by Peter, a student in my psychology class at Washington High School. I showed no interest at the time. Years later, a young man came to visit my ill sister in my home. He would come daily, when my sister was living with me. Each morning he would chant. He encouraged me to chant Nam-Myoho-Renge-Kyo. I immediately felt the effect of this chant. A peaceful feeling came over me like I had never had before. Within a few weeks, I began to have confidence and saw this as my actual proof of the power of Buddhism. I was no longer fear-based as I had been before. I made significant changes in my life. I overcame my fear of teaching dance and had one class that eventually became five. I built a room on top of my house, overcoming my fear of lack of money. I also introduced this practice to my daughter, Despina.

I first saw Daisaku Ikeda, the man who was to become my mentor and the president of our Buddhist organization, the Soka Gakkai International or SGI, at a convention in San Diego in 1972. He was so filled with love and strength, it permeated my life, weakening my hardened wall of protection. I immediately began to cry when I saw him and it continued for days. Not crying was part of the praise I had received from my mother so for me to actually be able to cry was a miracle. He talked about each of us creating a major transformation in our lives, which he called "human revolution." Then, he said, that would cause a major transformation of the entire world.

I know I would not be alive today if I had not found this incredible practice. My constant thoughts of suicide left me. My greatest benefit is that I have been able to transform so much of my own negativity into hope, appreciation, and compassion for others. I would never have thought that at 80 years old I could continue to make the impossible possible with total confidence, and that's what gives me the greatest joy. I love to introduce people to this practice because I love to see people do their human revolution.

Chapter 31, My Tumultuous Years: 1972-1982

When I was transferred to Lowell High School in June 1972, I was quite excited. I hoped I would finally be in an environment where homophobia would not be dominant as it was in my previous school. That was not to be. Once again, I faced the same karma. Not only were the other teachers homophobic, their actions of ignoring me and being totally non-supportive were scary to me as I was openly gay. My lover, Rita, brought me flowers right in front of my coworkers.

Lowell High School was the most competitive school in San Francisco as, at the time, you had to have straight As to be accepted. You were also required to maintain straight As. Needless to say, it was difficult for me to be part of that school. I did have one benefit. I was able to teach dance and have my own dance studio, which was gorgeous with lovely hardwood floors, stall bars and huge mirrors. It was my dream come true.

Because of the competitive environment, the Chinese students suffered greatly. They would come to me with such horrible rashes on their hands; their nerves affected them so deeply. I carried a first-aid kit with creams to help them through their suffering. It did help a little, but the competition was deadly.

I was not a trained ballet teacher like the preceding teacher, which gave the faculty another reason to dislike me. My training had been jazz and modern dance. I had an excellent education in both, and my principal and his wife, who had been a modern dancer, both liked me. I think that is why I was hired.

I had a great deal to offer the students. They loved my class and would come after school to practice. I taught the students techniques, then had them branch out with their own movements. That way, it was a creative process and not a follow-the-leader form of teaching. Many boys signed up for my class, and they loved it. I would find them on the basketball court or on the football field. They were quite creative in their movements, and I saw their potential.

In my second year at Lowell, I asked to have our dance production in the gymnasium as I wanted to have more space for the dances and a bigger audience. My department head denied me the request, but the principal heard of it and said I could perform in the gym. That went over horribly in the P.E. department. No one would even talk to me.

I did not mind the hostile environment as I was in heaven in my dance classes. The way my students were advancing was beyond my expectations, and that made me happy. I taught choreography after school so my students could begin to create their own dances, which they did beautifully. I never had any discipline problems. My students were totally involved and excited to be part of the creative adventure.

When we put on our first dance production in the gymnasium, my students were passionate about the creation of a theatre in the gym. We made a backdrop out of old white sheets sewn together with flip-tops from soda cans connected and hanging down from the top to the bottom of the painted sheets. That gave a shiny, glossy effect that everyone loved.

We had four dance productions and always had a full house. The students could not believe the applause we received at the end of each performance. I had 3 more great years at Lowell teaching dance. However, in my 4th year, I had one student named Lisa who could not stand me and made it known to everyone. To her, dance was ballet. We did not do ballet, so she thought my class had no value to her. I had told her to transfer out, which she refused to do. She would do the warm ups, then sit for the rest of class with her smeary, smug looks. When the semester ended, I had to give her a C for a final grade. She was furious, as that meant she had not maintained the straight As she needed to stay at Lowell.

In September, when I returned from my summer in Greece, I ran into a former student at the airport in Paris. She came running up to me asking if I had heard that Lisa had sued me to change her grade. I was shocked, yet I realized Lisa was a spoiled child who would go to any means to get her way. Furthermore, her father was a lawyer. So I had to face a year with a lawsuit. It was in newspapers all over the country because it was a precedent case. No other students had ever sued a teacher to change their grades.

My lawyer told me not to worry, but the school environment had changed. I no longer had my studio for dance. I had to share it with the sweaty wrestling team. They left such a stench! The horrible smell from those young male bodies made it almost impossible for me to teach my classes.

Lowell also became the favorite school for Asian students. They had such high grades that Lowell became mainly Asian. I had problems with my predominantly Asian class. These students were not creative in modern dance. They wanted to copy everything I did but were incapable creating anything on their own. They were left-brained kids, which was great for academics but not for a creative dance class.

There were too many obstacles piling up for me. In addition to the other teachers' hostility, the stench of the wrestling team, and the lack of creativity in my Asian students, Lisa was allowed to stay at Lowell even though she had lost the lawsuit.

I decided to transfer to another school. It made me so sad, though, when the gay and lesbian students organized their own club at the school and invited me to be their sponsor. I felt so privileged to be asked but knew my time at Lowell High School had come to an end. Sadly, I had to refuse even though they told me I had encouraged them to come out and to be themselves. I took this to be a wonderful farewell to 5 years of tremendous victory in my life and my creativity.

Just as I was leaving Lowell, I received a thank you letter from one of my students. I had taken her off the basketball court and helped her become a great dancer and choreographer. In her letter to me, she wrote that she had received a scholarship from Texas A.M. University for her abilities in dance. I still feel such gratitude and pride for my 5 years at Lowell High School.

While I was at Lowell, I had an incredible experience: one day I took my car in to have my radio fixed, and this young man comes up and sits next to me and starts having a conversation, asking me questions about my life. He was kind and personable—I felt very comfortable with him and after my car was ready and his car was to be finished the next day, I offered to take him to his hotel. He was fascinated when I told him that my daughter had a scholarship to ACT for acting.

When we arrived at his hotel he invited me up to his room for a drink and I was so taken with this man that I parked my car in the hotel garage and went up with him. When I walked in I was shocked: all the walls in the room had bookshelves, from the floor to the ceiling and books covered all the shelves. I asked, "Why do you have all these books?"

He told they were his best friend's. I questioned further, "Why?"

He told me when he was a child, he was too small in New York to go out in the streets, and his mother was afraid he would get beaten up by the other bigger boys. He had to read a book every week and than he had to act it out for his mother. When I asked what was he doing in San Francisco, he said he was making a film in Stockton. I asked him, "Who are you?" When he said Al Pacino, I said you do not look like him; he said it all had to do with makeup. He *did* look like the man in the film *Scarecrow*. Anyway, after we had a drink, he began his academy-award seduction of me. I tried to leave three times but he was so seductive I could not resist him. After he got me in his bed I was shocked at how he was this wam-bam-thank-you-ma'am kind of guy—as soon as it began, it was over. I dressed and was about to leave and he wanted my phone number; I saw he had a lot of women's names in his little address book. His sincere desire for me was seductive; he made me feel special.

When I went home I could not believe what I had just done. I called Laz, an old boyfriend from New York, and told him what had just happened and he laughed and said "That is what all the guys do in New York. They have bets between each other of how many women they can seduce each day."

Chapter 32, 1982-1983: My Sabbatical Year

I was so grateful to receive my sabbatical in 1982, and I felt like I deserved it after being in schools and struggling so hard with other teachers and never fitting in for 15 years. My daughter Roxanne felt safe to me living with her boyfriend in New York, so I knew it was time for me to explore the Far East.

Since I had so much encouragement from my friend Marge who had traveled alone in the Far East, I felt I also could do it. She had told me I would not have to worry about Asian men as they would not harass me but would cater to me, and that they did for my entire trip.

I flew out of San Francisco to Japan where I wanted to visit my Buddhist organization's head temple and have a month traveling around Japan. On the plane, I met a friendly Japanese man who talked to me about his country for the entire journey. He was full of wonderful information about places I should stay and eat, as well as visit. I was shocked when he offered to take me to a hotel after we landed. I thought, for sure, he would want to stay with me; but, much to my amazement, he took me to my room, thanked me for the wonderful time he had with me on the plane, said goodnight, and left. This was my first surprise about the kindness of Asian men. In my previous experiences, any lengthy conversation with a man was always followed by the expectation of going to bed with him, especially if he was paying for your hotel.

I loved traveling in Japan alone, but most people were not friendly. I guess they had good reason after the U.S. bombed the hell out of them in 1945. Nonetheless, the members of my Buddhist organization, the SGI, were extremely friendly. I could connect with them everywhere in Japan and often spent the night in their homes. It amazed me when an entire family would all sleep on the floor in one room. In the morning, they would roll up their futons and blankets and put them under the benches that were along two walls. I never felt crowded in these homes as the Japanese really understand the concept of keeping your own space.

Traveling on the bullet train was awesome. I had never experienced such speed on the ground. All the people were reading or eating rather than talking. The train did make a lot of noise, so it was difficult to carry on a conversation.

Nagasaki and Hiroshima were the first places I wanted to see. There is an incredible museum in Hiroshima that depicts the disaster of the atomic bomb the U.S. dropped in 1945. As I entered the museum, the smell of burning flesh and smoke surrounded me. Then I began to see models of all the dead bodies that looked so real, as well as survivors with horrible defects all over their bodies. The colors were dark and scary. There were sounds of people screaming. It was a horror show as the exhibit wanted visitors to feel what they felt from the bombing. I left the museum after forty minutes crying my eyes out. It was so powerful and real. I think everyone in the world should see this museum to understand the horrors caused by nuclear war.

I loved the Japanese food, so tasty and not at all filling like heavy American food. Everything is individually and finely prepared, never tasting the same in each restaurant I visited. I found plum wine, which I drank all over the Asia, as it was sweet and inexpensive. The wine helped me sleep, as I had developed insomnia traveling alone.

The Japanese gardens were breathtaking with many flowers that were new to me and an abundance of colorful fish. The people took wonderful pride in keeping their country clean, I never saw litter anywhere. If it had not been for staying in the SGI Buddhist members' homes, I would have been extremely lonely. For the entire month, I did not sit at tables like I was used to in the U.S.; everything was prepared on tables on the floor. The cooking was done in a separate room except when the people only had one room, then they cooked on the table, sitting on the floor.

In many places in the streets, I found people chanting Nam Myoho Renge Kyo to small altars which had statues of foxes or snakes in them, much to my surprise. That is not the way I was taught to practice Buddhism. I went to many temples as I wanted to see their beautiful grounds and buildings. My trip to Japan was a grand beginning of my journey in Asia.

I had to stay a week in Hong Kong waiting to get a visa to China, the communist government was just beginning to open to foreigners. I made friends with an American couple, Fred and Jenny, who was also going to China. They were absolute loves and took such good care of me. After a month of not speaking to a single American, I was delighted.

We did tours together. Climbing the hilly streets of Hong Kong reminded me of San Francisco. The harbor had many strange-looking big boats, narrow and colorful—bright red, yellow, and green. I did not like the food in Hong Kong, but I found out later there are two styles of cooking in China: Cantonese and Szechuan. I preferred the Szechuan way of cooking as it had more choices of hot spicy food, and I liked the way they quick-fried and steamed the vegetables. The Cantonese food had no flavor to me, and I did not find it tasty at all. Once I learned the difference, I could order what I liked. Even though I was born and raised in San Francisco, I had never known this difference. Most of the restaurants in San Francisco are of the Cantonese culture.

After the week was up, I received my visa and was off to China on the train ride to Canton. I met a man from Chicago, a lawyer who was born in China. I was so grateful when he took me under his wing as there were no guide books. I was guided only through the many wonderful, helpful people I met.

He took me to the elegant Swan Hotel. I could not believe there was a hotel like that in such a deprived, poor culture. I saw people and supplies being carried around in carts or buggies on wheels. The communists still held block meetings every week to keep the people under control. However, capitalism was beginning to be felt as I saw in the Swan Hotel that was owned by some wealthy men, the lawyer informed me. The hotel was huge—a first-class, modern hotel with gorgeous plants and statues from different eras in China. The food was also delicious Szechuan with spices I had never tasted before. I swam in the hotel swimming pool, which no one used. At that time, local women and men had no swimming attire. Throughout China, I noticed that no one ever swam in places I found ideal. During all my travels in China, I was constantly met with nasty sneers from the women. I saw all the people dressed only in navy blue, black, or brown except for the actors in the theatre. Only there were they allowed to wear bright colors.

I was definitely an odd ball, but I wanted to see China. I found my way through many places of interest, such as Guangzhou. I stayed in a hotel there that felt like an old mansion in the southern United States. I slept with huge netted tenting over my bed that covered and protected me from all the mosquitoes. Visiting China's famous Terracotta Warriors was awesome. To build a hundred statues of soldiers and for them to have survived underground for so many years is something unbelievable.

I continued through China without seeing anyone other than the Chinese people. I was the only American traveling alone and the only one who traveled on trains. All the other tourists traveled on buses. On the trains, the women stared at me with such anger throughout my trip. I was prepared for this, and it did not bother me. Traveling in China was exhilarating to me.

Xian was one of the most interesting, yet horrifying places in China. Traveling down the Yangtze River in a boat, I saw many dead female newborns floating down the river. Girls were often killed at birth because poor families could not afford to feed and clothe them just to have them join another family when they were old enough to help out. All value was placed on boys. After that frightening experience, I was still able to enjoy my trip as I saw the gorgeous, tall, black mountains that are part of the Dangla mountain range. These are the mountains often seen in Chinese paintings. It was a breathtaking experience.

I never saw people interacting. Everyone walked rapidly. It was easy to sense that the people had no personal freedom and that the Communist party had total control over them. Mao controlled his people with fear and great punishment.

When I went to Wuwan, I visited a museum where I saw a photo of Zhou Enlai. He looked insane, but later became a hero for the people. He had been Mao's right hand man, but he fought for human rights when fear and punishment were synonyms in a Communist country like China.

Shanghai was a shocking exception in China. All the people there were dressed like westerners. A man proposed to me while I was there because he wanted desperately to go to the United States. I went to the theatre and could not believe what I had seen on the stage. The people were dressed in such elegant, colorful, and interesting clothes. Even though I didn't understand what they were saying, I was so surprised by the contrast of these incredibly bright hues in front of me from the bland tones that painted the world outside the theatre.

My most humane experience came when I was in Beijing. I had arrived late at night to this city where no one spoke English. Thank goodness men always took care of me. I was taken to another elegant hotel, but the man working at the desk said "Sorry, no rooms," in his broken English. However, this good-hearted man gave me a cot located in a little room behind his desk. I was so grateful to have a place to sleep.

At the time of my travels, most people in China's cities, including Beijing, used bicycles for transportation. I had never seen so many bikes. The next big surprise was that in every park, every morning, hundreds of people were doing the national Tai Chi exercises together, all in rhythm. When I left China on a boat to return to Hong Kong, I slept the entire trip. My six weeks in China had been exhausting, but unforgettable. Pollution had not yet overtaken the entire Far East as it has now.

Nepal 1982

I was tired of the Asian coldness in the weather and in the people. I really wanted to be in a warm, loving country that would please all my senses, so I caught the first plane out of Hong Kong to Nepal where the weather, food, and people were fantastic.

As the plane landed in Kathmandu, the passengers exited the plane single file down the stairs. In the airport, my feet landed on soft lovely rugs. Everything was covered with colored rugs, filled with sand from people's feet. There were no cement or tile floors. Immediately, I was overwhelmed with the lovely mixed smells of spices, incense, and manure from animals. Everyone had on long dresses, including men, who wore long gowns covering their western suits to keep them clean.

The people in Nepal were extremely friendly and warm. They could not do enough for me, finding me a nice, safe place for a very reasonable price. I always felt safe and completely at home there.

On my first night there, I noticed that people used candles for light. Electricity was a scarce commodity, and most homes were heated by wood. Generators were used in restaurants and stores for light.

I woke up happily the second morning to the sounds of Kathmandu. People were parading in the dirt streets with their monkeys on their backs. With painted faces they marched, laughing and joking all the way. Elephants with colored streaks on their faces and trunks, and cows, too, marched with the people and their monkeys. It was common to see monkeys swinging from tree to tree. There was some kind of celebration almost every day as the cultures of Nepal and India have many holy days or holidays. I asked other tourists about the painting of the animals and was told this was done to attract certain gods for their protection.

I loved all the food. I can still smell the pita bread, with many spicy vegetables and mainly lamb meat. Beef is not eaten because cows are sacred to the people. Nepal had a lively atmosphere, not loud but extremely busy. There were many Muslims, and the Muslim women's faces were covered with burqas. I do not appreciate how married women were treated as property belonging to their husbands, that is why their faces are always covered. The young girls, however, wore long dresses, their hair flowing freely in the wind.

Children went to school for four hours, five days a week. They sat on dirt floors that were highly polished. I sat on them, and they felt like a fine cut of wood. Trees in most of Asia have huge roots that bulge out of the ground looking like a variety of sculptured abstractions.

I was taken to the Himalayas by a nice young man. We sat on top of a bus as there was no more room inside. A mother sitting next to me was beating her child, and I could not believe how everyone ignored her. I asked the young man, "Why do the women here beat their children so easily?" He replied that it was their custom.

I stayed in a mud hut in the Himalayas and loved it as the women were so friendly. The men were not, and they looked at me suspiciously. The women loved to dance together. They would always pull me into their circle, laughing and singing while we danced. Climbing in the Himalayas was an ecstatic experience. Snow was everywhere, but I did not feel cold. After being there for a few days, the high altitude began to affect me. I returned to Kathmandu happy to have had that wonderful experience in those majestic mountains.

I met some English and German students and hung out with them for a few days. They were so interesting as they had just come from India, and they shared many stories of places I should visit. After my two weeks in Nepal, I found a bus going to Delhi, India, with many of the foreign students and other travelers. I was a bit homesick as I'd had no contact with anyone from my family for three months. Phoning home at that time was almost impossible. I knew as soon as I arrived in a big city like Delhi, I would find a phone and be able to connect with my family. I could hardly wait.

India

After seeing the life of Gandhi in a film that won many academy awards in 1980, I began reading every book I could find about this incredible man. That was my motivating desire to go to India to see where this unbelievable human being had lived and won the country's independence from the British. He changed the course of his country with his non violent movement against the British Empire.

Delhi was without a doubt the strangest big city I had ever seen. My first glimpses of it were huge white buildings built by the

British contrasted by small three-wheel motorcycles driving all over the sidewalks and people walking in the streets. English rule of the road obviously had not reached India in that way. All the women wore lovely long saris of many different colors. The colors I found in that city stimulated my senses constantly; the smells of curry and the many other herbs kept me in a state of fascination.

When I arrived to the Ganges River, I was shocked when a large group of men rolled out on wood platforms with wheels underneath them as they sat up begging for money. They had no teeth, some had six fingers, three eyes, they were all disfigured. I could not believe how everyone bathed, washed their clothes, and drank the same water from the Ganges River.

The British left a magnificent railway system that made it possible to cover a great deal of miles in a short period of time. On my way to Rajasthan, I looked out the window for a moment and saw a man lying on the other track with his head next to him. This freaked me out so much I had to get off at the next station. I was so upset. There was another woman on the train from Germany who had the same reaction as I did and we both hugged each other as we were in such a state of shock. We stayed together for a week recovering from the horrible incident we both had experienced. She spoke very little English and I did not speak German but our trauma kept us together until we felt strong enough to go off on our journeys alone. I stayed in many places but forgot their names. Every town and city had gold statues of Gandhi in the center of the town.

The food I found in India was to me the best in the world as far as nutrition, it was very tasty, spicy and delicious. I used to eat with my hands when I was a child and my mother would say, "You are not in India," so I was very happy in India eating with my hands. The smell of wood burning was another strong sensual experience as dead people daily are incinerated and then their ashes are thrown into the Ganges River.

I then took a train to Sri Lanka. Sensuality, color, smells of incense, spices, and the sweat of the people keep you awake and alive as everything in India is intense. The number of people was something awesome. Though the caste system has it such that the lowest, the untouchables, live in the streets, they are very clean and they have their space and respect. I could not believe they did not look like our American homeless. These people wear clean and wore neat clothes; women wore their saris and men wore shorts and clean shirts. Everyone wears sandals and the children were well behaved. Because the people believe in Karma, stealing is rare.

In Sri Lanka, I was once again greeted by huge elephants, whose noses were all painted in different colors with young handsome men dressed only in mid cloth covering their groin. Monkeys were always hanging from trees as in Kathmandu. I was fortunate to find a woman who spoke and taught English. The extremely kind woman who's name I cannot recall, had a room for rent and I spent a week with her finding out about Sri Lanka. The constant war going between the Tamils and the Hindu was difficult to understand. I saw an amazing show of Shadow Dancing by puppets who were hung by strings and manipulated by these strings behind a sheet with a light glaring at them from the back of the theater. I have a doll hanging on my wall in my kitchen as a reminder of this magical moment. I was never lonely in India because everyday was a new discovery.

Watching men run through fire and dance in and out of the fire was another memorable moment. Every day was like going to a living theatre, sometimes absurd and other times fascinating. I wanted to stay longer but I had to go onto other countries.

Next, I flew to Bangkok to see the city of gold and all the many Buddhas. I arrived late at night and did not know where to go; this young man said he was going to a hostel and asked me if I would like to join him. Out of desperation, I said yes. I knew Thailand had a terrible drug reputation but I had never seen anything like what I was about to encounter. It was a house full of young people out of their minds from drug abuse; it was late and I decided I had to stay. They gave me room in the cellar and when I went to lay down, a rat was next to me. I covered my head and laid there until dawn, then fled with terror. I ran out into the daylight and thank goodness I ran into two American men who took me to their hotel to shower and eat. I was hysterical. I decided I did not want to travel in Thailand and caught the next train out of the cold city.

I got on a train where I could sleep as I was exhausted from my four months of travel with very little rest. The countryside of Thailand was quite beautiful and the people on the train were constantly giving me food. I could not get over how many Americans were in Thailand but I knew it was because of the freedom of drugs in the country at that time. Many men had their pinky finger with an extremely long nail which was used to sniff cocaine. I saw it on a number of men from many different countries.

When we arrived in Kuala Lumpur, Malaysia, it felt like another world: everything was extremely clean and orderly. Being a Muslim country, it had very strict laws and rules, women had their heads and face covered and everything was so pristine, but I did not find the Muslim people friendly. I was fortunate to find a lovely hostel and wanted to stay for some time. The problem was that my Buddhist organization had to be underground, as the Muslim religion was the only one accepted in Malaysia. I met an SGI member there and she told me it was not a place I should travel, nor would it be very interesting alone. The Muslim men are not like other Asian men, apparently, they are very aggressive. So after a week I got on another train and went to Singapore. This country, which is one big city on an island, is so clean you can eat off of the streets. I loved the food but it was too rigid and felt like the west.

I called home and my daughter told me she was ill and pregnant, and asked me to come home. My trip to the Far East was cut short by six months, I had to go home and take care of my daughter. My sabbatical was for a year abroad, now I would have to go to school for six months to keep my sabbatical paycheck every month. When I arrived home my daughter said she had miscarried.

I was glad to be home after six months in Asia, it was a most memorable trip that I shall never forget because it was so foreign and interesting. My senses were stimulated daily with the sounds, colors and all customs that were quite different from the U.S. India without a doubt was my favorite country, a daily sensual delight that made me want to return. It is impossible for me even to think of traveling now to India as it has become the most populated country in the world besides China.

The next week I enrolled at San Francisco City College to take art classes. My sabbatical required that I either study or travel. I had always wanted to study art as most of my lovers had been artists and I wanted to explore this world for myself. I studied drawing, art history, and painting, which I loved.

Chapter 33, Teaching Around SF

That fall I began teaching at Balboa high school and it was great because I was going to have my own dance studio, I was excited. The problem was that once again I would replace a favorite dance teacher; she taught ballet and all of the students loved her. This was the same problem I had at Lowell high school, where the students wanted their former teacher back who stressed ballet. My karma was once again present. Thank goodness I had some students who loved that I taught jazz and modern dance. My star dancer was a drug addict who performed like Michael Jackson. I would have to go to his home and bribe him with food to get him to perform as we needed him so badly. I did not have any male dancers to replace him, this was not a memorable time. I was tired of teaching and dealing with difficult students who wanted to fool around. I also taught art, math and physical education during that ten year period at Balboa.

I was then transferred to International Studies Academy, and taught only physical education and history for three years. The students at ISA wanted to go to school except for a few Latino students. One terrifying day, I saw two young boys hanging out the building windows, showing off to the other students.

When I had climbed the stairs of ISA, as it was called, I saw large paintings of Martin Luther King, Gandhi, and Abraham Lincoln. I made a determination that I wanted to see a painting of our SGI president Daisaku Ikeda on these walls. I did accomplish this. The principal was Chinese and a former captain in the army. The Iraq war had begun. I was one of the teachers against the war, and the principle did not care for me. He was always coming into my class unannounced glaring at me with a frown on his face. However, I invited him to our Buddhist Culture center to see what our Buddhist practice was all about. Our organization is fighting for world peace: for example, every year, Daisaku Ikeda writes a peace proposal to the United Nations, and has held dialogues all over the world with many national leaders. Our principal eventually did come and our SGI-USA general director had a special meeting with him, where he learned about our efforts for peace. He was so impressed by the exhibit at our center and his dialogue with our general director. By the time I left ISA, a mural of Rosa Parks and Daisaku Ikeda, based on a photo taken during their encounter, was painted on the school grounds.

After teaching history and physical education for three years at ISA, I decided to take the Golden Handshake, which was offered to teachers who had over 20 years teaching where they would give us three extra years on our retirement in return for three years of master teaching. That was a joke: master teaching basically meant I would help teachers correct papers and clean up after the teachers went home. I loved teaching, my problem was my many female bosses. I just did not fit into the public school system as I was not socially active with them. I was too busy with my many lovers and my Buddhist practice.

Chapter 34, My Many Relationships with Unavailable Women

I must not forget my many relations with women from 1972 to 2016. There were so many women and they all taught me a great deal. I can never forget them because they each were very special and some were very painful. I was to have an abundant number of relations in my 30s and after up until I retired from teaching when I was 57 in 1992. For many years, I explored men and women: when a relationship with a woman would be on the down end, I would go with men since they were so easy for me to handle (except for Julius). Women were my big challenge, I always picked unavailable ones. I never realized until I reached my 70s that maybe because my parents were not emotionally available for me that I only knew these patterns of behavior of unavailable people.

Kim, a good-looking black woman who had an afro when I met her in the 70s, was the only person with whom I was ever able to have casual sex with; it wasn't filled with the search for her to fix me—I was never addicted to her. She dressed elegantly and was well-groomed. A Gemini, she was a great listener, and I sure did need a good listener as I was suffering so much with my drug-addict daughters. She was a school counselor when I met her at George Washington High, and we became friends immediately. The school was in such a disarray with the African American students rebelling that her presence as a counselor was healthy and supportive for them. Around the time the principal permitted me to introduce psychology to the curriculum, Kim began to teach a class in Sociology. We became friends and great traveling buddies—since we both had the summers off we would take trips together. We traveled to Canada, the Middle East, and some of the Caribbean together. She was fun and we shared time together with no problems. I am very grateful we are still friends as I write my memoir.

Barbara was my next lover: she was one of my student's older sister, around the same age as myself. She was a very bright woman who knew how to seduce me, and that she did with great style. She knew how to satisfy me sexually, she was an Aquarian—a brilliant innovator and very smart, but needed a lot of attention. She taught art at Chico State University, a few hours northeast of San Francisco. Barbara was the first person who opened up the world of painting to me. Liz, my first lover, had told me dance was my expression and not painting, and I had trusted her since she was a famous artist. Barbara would encourage me to try, she told me, "Pick up the paintbrush!"

That was just what I needed to open up my love for painting. She was a talented woman who helped me with my dance productions, painting a great backdrop for my show. It was difficult for us to see each other, as I was worn out from teaching during the week at Lowell High and then driving hours up to Chico. We had a short intense six months and a dreadful three-month trip to Europe together, with my two daughters.

During those six months, my daughters were both in Europe, and I missed them terribly. Then entered Rita, a Scorpio with her two beautiful daughters. She was a good-looking, dykey woman with beautiful seductive brown eyes. I met her at a Buddhist meeting, and after a few weeks, she invited me to her house. When she came up and kissed me on the mouth just like Liz had done, she knew what she was doing—that was her Scorpio way of seducing me. I was hooked to her sexually and I adored her lovely daughters.

I traveled to Europe for the summer with Barbara as we had bought chartered plane tickets. It was a painful experience as I was really in love with Rita. I felt horrible but sex between us was always great so that was the only way we could connect. We met up with Despina and Roxanne in Paris. They smoked pot daily with Barbara and had a good time. I was lost in lust for Rita. When we returned home, Rita was waiting for me at the airport and Barbara was so upset she dropped a very expensive bottle of Italian liquor. I had really hurt her and I felt terrible. She naturally would have nothing to do with me after our breakup.

Rita moved into my home and after six months she started drinking. I knew something was wrong. One day she brought her new friend home and I could tell immediately that they were very connected. A few weeks later, I came home and found them in bed together. I reacted by bringing a man home which made Rita move out within a week.

My dearest friends, Ruth and Judy, by now had a dating business and would host a party every month to help gay women connect. At one of their many parties a few months after Rita left, still feeling the pain from the breakup, I walked in and I immediately saw this very tall gorgeous woman that I liked. She had a stance about her that demanded attention and she certainly always got it. Curly black hair, big brown eyes and a loving smile that Libra's are famous for. Her name was C.K. We got into a heated argument as I said I thought Paris was a feminine city and London was a masculine city. C.K. said "No, Paris is masculine and London is feminine," and

I just dismissed her. A week later C.K. called me, I was shocked: she liked me. She was very arrogant so I was not impressed, really, but she had a very persuasive side to her; besides being good looking, she was a charmer. I loved her creative spirit as she was a photographer and immediately invited me to her dark room to teach me how to develop film.

We became lovers soon after but I never felt C.K. was available, as she was a heavy drinker. She would have blackouts and do outrageous things like lay on the hood of my car as I was driving. I was hooked, in love with her and I wanted to live with her. We decided to buy a house together. I loved the Bayview district in San Francisco as it is warm and the view of the bay was exciting. The Bayview at that time was basically people of color and I loved their warmth and friendliness. The day we went to look at a house, C.K. was drunk. I saw the value of the house and decided we should buy it. This began our creative adventure together.

That summer C.K.'s son, Justin, came to visit us from Germany where he lived with his father. The three of us tore the roof off of the house to begin building a second story. We found Mark, a builder, who was a student at UC Berkeley studying architecture. He was a creative genius: his ideas for how to make the second floor 25' x 35' with unique, slanted windows that capture more sunlight with 2 x 6 beams jutting from the wall to the center with a steel plate holding them together were simply marvelous. This type of ceiling made it earthquake proof and aesthetically pleasing to the eye. I still love what he created for the house. It is truly a work of art.

Mark and C.K. would stay up all night drinking and getting stoned, making a ton of noise. I would get very upset and did not know what to do. Then, out of know where, C.K got an offer for a job in Germany managing a women's theatrical group. I thought this would be a good time for us to have a break from our relationship. I did not hear from C.K for quite a while. Finally, she calls me and tells me she has a new girlfriend, I went crazy with envy, but months later I accepted it. I finished rebuilding the house and then rented it out. I moved back to my home in the Castro.

In the meantime, I met Gail who was a very handsome, daring woman and a famous organizer of women's events in San Francisco. She was smart, attractive, with gorgeous blue eyes and starling white hair. When she invited me to her home I could not believe her actions as she grabbed my crotch and said, "What would it take to get you in my bed?" I was shocked, but fascinated by her boldness. A true

Scorpio. She knew how to go after what she wanted. I took off my straight-jacket of shyness by using alcohol. It was she who introduced me to drinking hard liquor—I found it made sex much more intense. I would go to her house every week to get drunk and have sex. Gail had two Afghan dogs who I felt were her lovers. I had never seen anyone be so intimate with their animals as she was. This relationship got me through the horrible time breaking up with C.K., which went on for quite a few years until I met Louise.

Louise was one of the most popular lesbians in the city. She was a film editor for the television station Channel 4. A very exotic woman, not beautiful but handsome, with intense brown eyes that made her a great seducer. I shall never forget the way she looked at me when I met her at a party, it was like she looked right through me and saw my essence. I fell in love with her—just like everyone else. Even C.K. did too. What a time that was: C.K. wanted to be with Louise and Louise loved me but I was too insecure to be with her. She told me that I was the only woman whom she permitted to make love to her. She had always been the aggressor, and an alcoholic.

I recently learned that C.K. has Alzheimer's, and Louise and Gail both died years ago from throat cancer, all three were heavy smokers.

My daughters were still heavily into drugs, but finally Despina entered into the 12-step program with Alcoholics Anonymous. I went to a meeting with her, and there I was to meet Ana Maria. Immediately, I felt like I knew her from a past life with her heavy German accent, a stocky build, shining blue eyes, and long blond hair blowing in the wind on winter day. She was a very strong woman with people surrounding her. When I glanced over to acknowledge her, I wanted to know her.

After that, I attended AA meetings religiously. I hooked up with Ana Maria like a sinking ship. I felt I could not stop drinking, but she gave me the confidence that I could do it. At night, I would call her and soon I lost the desire to drink. I became addicted to her. I was so dependent on her that I wanted to give her whatever she wanted. She said she wanted to live in the country so when my dear friends Ruthie and Judy invited me to visit them in their new home in Healdsburg, I took Ana Maria with me.

I loved Healdsburg immediately. Judy and Ruthie drove us up this beautiful angular tree-covered road on South Fitch Mountain, with a large forested hill looming over the town. I fell in love with the winding road, covered with trees on either side, with the river below. Passing many houses that were for sale, nothing caught my eye. Out of nowhere we pass this handwritten "For Sale" sign on this old, decrepit house, and I immediately became interested. When we stopped to check it out, a strange looking Russian man invited us into the house. It had a bit of movement as I walked across the floor. At the back of the room, the windows looked out over the most incredible view of the river shimmering like diamonds from the sun on the water; the distance before me was breathtaking, mesmerizing me with the vista of layered mountains reminding me of the Southern Coast of France. The house felt like it was falling in the river, "Such a disaster," I thought to myself, but something pulled me to it. I knew this house had to be mine. Especially when I ran down the four flights of broken stairs and jumped into the river with my clothes on, I knew I had to have this house no matter what.

Ana Maria did not like the idea of me having to rebuild a house. She wanted to live in the country, however, and I was so dependent on her for my recovery from drinking that I bought her a small house trailer and a car, just to keep her in my life. I sold my home in the Castro to fix up the four-story disaster in Healdsburg and moved back into my home in the Bayview after I bought out C.K.'s share.

However, I soon became tired of Ana Maria not liking my Buddhist practice. She was into The Goddess as her spiritual practice and I did not appreciate her spiritual practice either. She believed in The Goddess but her behavior was so absurd: I could not see a goddess in her, though other women in AA certainly did. We parted ways soon after that.

Once again, I went to a party given by my dear friends Ruthie and Judy who had so many lesbian friends; it was only natural that I was to meet my next lover, Marilyn. I immediately was drawn to her gorgeous big smile and her warmth, a large woman who had a sexy large butt. I proudly showed her pictures of my beautiful disaster of a house on the Russian River and she too, loved it. I was hooked: I had met someone who loved my new home. Marilyn was breaking up with another woman but the chemistry between us was so strong—we soon became lovers after she gave me an incredible massage, which was just one of her many gifts. She was a hypnotherapist and encouraged me to study to become one after my Roxanne died.

I went to the mountains to study hypnotherapy for a month. I was not as intuitive as Marilyn and used hypnotherapy on friends occasionally. I was such a sexual animal and Marilyn was not. It seems our karma was so strong, we remained unhappily together for years. Marilyn and I both had a seed of hatred toward each other that seemed to grow with time. The desire to forget how we once were and realizing how to let her go was the strongest pain.

Marilyn did make it possible for me to finish rebuilding my home: she was from Sonoma and knew many people who were in the building business. At the time I was teaching in San Francisco and I would come up on weekends. Marilyn was into my project and helped me get a permit which was almost impossible because of a septic tank being inside the house, but with our shared focus we were able to find a solution. We found a man who had just moved here from Oregon who showed us how we could get the permit. He explained that since it's a four-story house and though the top floor was the only one standing, even if it was shaking, we could rebuild the top floor and everything below would be classified as the foundation. After the final inspections, we could put walls into the three floors below and have a four-story home. We were so excited that after two years we were able to finally move forward.

I had introduced Marilyn to my Buddhist practice, and felt there was a spiritual bond between us that I had never had before. I thought we could change our karma together, but when my daughter Roxanne committed suicide, I became very needy which she could not respond to because of her health issues and we became more separated because of it.

A few years ago, I was taking a memoir writing class and my teacher suddenly retired. By unfortunate coincidence (though nothing is coincidence), Marilyn became the teacher and she refused to permit me to be in her class. I was enraged, filled with hurt and anger and outright insulted. I could not understand her feelings, but time has a wonderful healing effect, I no longer care and I have a better teacher who has encouraged me much more than Marilyn would ever have.

Love is such a strange creature: it has a life of its own. I realized the desire to forget Marilyn was the strongest inducement for remembering her. I bit my tongue pouring out through the bleeding wounds of my aching heart. Now when I see her at our Buddhist center, I once again feel she is such an important part of my life and I treasure the memory of her. I have learned that I can be in love with more than one woman and not judge myself, love is what the world needs more of and that is what is lacking—greed, anger, and stupidity rule this sad earth.

I was then to meet Josefina whom I have been with for 25 years. She is a very intelligent, good looking woman, with sparkling brown eyes and gorgeous curly hair that is now almost white, which I love. She is a culturally-refined woman who was in the radio and television business in Mexico, who had come to San Francisco in the 70s on a scholarship. We had seen each other briefly at parties in the the 70s and 80s but in 1994, after my daughter's death, I was desperate to be with someone available. Josefina and I are quite compatible because we do not live together. I see her on some weekends and we talk on the phone twice a day. She, too, is a Buddhist. My entire family loves her so it is easy, and even though we have struggles, we have learned through our practice to go through the hard times. She is the only person I have been with that I can be totally myself—good, bad and whatever I need to be.

We have had a hard time for many years as I was hung up on Marilyn. Josefina's patience and our many trips to Mexico and South America have helped us to stay together. I have been studying Spanish ever since I retired, and meeting Josefina stimulated me a great deal to continue studying. It was not until I began watching the Spanish *telenovelas* that I became better able to communicate.

What is so interesting to me is that not until I started to write my memoir, which Josefina had stimulated me to do, did I never realize that my sexual addiction came from my father's sexual attraction to me. I think I felt unconsciously that my value as a human animal was sex, as that is what my father had always told me.

Recently, my daughter and I were passing Liz's home. The door was open. Despina said to me "I want to see Liz." She jumped out of the car and I sat there stunned as I knew Liz would never accept seeing me as she had told me 45 years previously. I waited in the car feeling very sad and hurt that this woman who had really created me—I would never had finished college without her, leading to my destiny as a teacher and able to retire with a salary I could live on for the rest of my life, who cared for me more than my own mother—denied me entry into her home. All I could do was cry. I wish she would see me. She is 96, in a wheelchair and has a hospital bed; she did ask about me but told my daughter, "I am afraid to see her." As Gabriel Garcia Marquez said, "The heart's memory eliminates the bad and magnifies the good."

Out of nowhere on July 22, 2016, I become obsessed wanting to see Liz—who's real name is Betty Guy—it was like a thunderbolt hit me in my heart, just like when I first met her. The next day I called my dear friend Kim in San Francisco telling her I would like to go the museum of Modern Art with her and she asked me if I had heard Betty Guy had died. I could not believe what she had just said. I almost fainted with shock because Betty had been on my mind all that day of her death, July 22nd, and I began to cry with the loss of her like I had never experienced before. I read in the newspaper that she had been born in 1920 but why had she always told me she was born in 1926, why had she lied to me about her age? Betty had lied about not being a lesbian and would never say we were lovers, such a tragedy, to live a life of such denial all because of her need to be famous, and that she was. The Queen of England has one of her many paintings. John Steinbeck inspired her to write and publish in 1992 about their long friendship. Betty's talents were immense as she also played the piano with such skill and ease.

I grieved for Betty the rest of the month crying—I had never even cried for my parents when they passed. Betty not seeing me for all those years did not remove the passion and appreciation I have for her. She is now within me and never shall we be separated. I have constant flashbacks of our rich life together. Looking into her eyes at a concert was an immediate rush, or our many trips to Europe; we were inseparable for many years, and now we shall never be apart because she is alive in my memory. We are one forever.

Chapter 35, Retirement: 1992

I shall never forget the day of my retirement: I was ecstatic with joy, I had looked forward to this day for such a long time. After teaching for 27 years, I was finally free to do what I wanted to do, which was to travel, and go back to school to study art and Spanish. I took every art class available at Santa Rosa Junior College and San Francisco City College. Studying art was something I had wanted to do for years because Betty had told me I was not an artist which made me want to study art after I retired. Barbara had also encouraged me. I loved painting classes, life-drawing, and especially drawing those gorgeous naked bodies who loved to pose for the art students.

Sculpting was another favorite of mine and I have all my work now in my home for me to appreciate that I can be an artist, maybe not famous but I can express myself, which Betty did not want me to do. I loved to get my hands all squashed up in wet muddy clay in that sculpturing class; I felt like I would like to stay in the class forever but we were only permitted to take the class for a semester.

When I took a Spanish class at Santa Rosa Jr. College, I knew I needed an immersion class where I would be in a Spanish-speaking country. I heard from a friend that Antigua, Guatemala was a lovely small town that catered to people who wanted to learn Spanish and was extremely inexpensive. Before that trip, I had always wanted to be a man. I signed up for a class that centered transgender folks at San Francisco City College as soon as I retired. San Francisco has always been very progressive and I'm sure it was the only college offering such as a class at that point in time. The focus of the class was on studying people who had transitioned and everyone in that class was either interested in transitioning or were fascinated by the subject. When I entered that room, it was a shimmering moment. The teacher was transitioning into a man, they looked so sick they could hardly stand and walked with a limp. After the class was over I asked them why they were so ill and all they could say was "male hormones are difficult for some women." It was a powerful life-changing moment. After watching the teacher for the entire five months, I realized I was not going to do that to my body. I would remain a lesbian.

Chapter 36, Travels

In September 1992, I invited my significant other at the time, Marilyn, to go with me to Guatemala. We planned to stay for six months. We found a nice home to stay, each of us had our own room and we were served breakfast and a meal at one in the afternoon as that is the time for the main meal in the region. Our hosts were Maria, a large woman with a missing eye, and Juan, her little husband who came up to her shoulders. They had a well-off son named Tomas who had two wives and two children from each wife. The Catholic church denies divorce, so it was difficult to eat the mid day meal each Tuesday not knowing which one of Tomas' families would be present.

The school we attended was fun as the woman who ran the school, Rosa, who was extremely friendly and kind, loved to teach us how the Guatemalan people prepared their food. Rice and beans were the main course with a variety of vegetables, and very little meat as it was so expensive.

We had a memorable weekend on the seashore, sleeping in hammocks which I found very uncomfortable. I loved the people, they were warm and friendly—the Mayan people are more reserved and stay to themselves, probably because they are distrustful of outsiders. They live outside of Antigua living in large areas on smooth earth that has turned extremely hard but comfortable.

The Mayan men work in the fields and the women are great weavers and make lovely materials with a vibrant variety of colors: blankets, skirts, shirts, and purses that they sell to the tourists who come to Guatemala. The Spanish school we went to had a cooking class every Friday and we would all go to the outdoor market and buy food for our meal, our teacher would give us instructions on how to cook—it was educational and fun.

I loved when it was someone's birthday in the neighborhood and the neighbors would hire a group of singers and a guitarist who would come at dawn and sing happy birthday to the loved one.

I took colorful buses of red and blue throughout the country on weekends. Because Guatemala is such a small, rich, and colorful country it is easy to travel in a short period of time. The only place that I did not like was Guatemala City, it is poverty stricken with hundreds of young children out in the street begging. Their clothes were full of holes and they were very dirty with a horrible musty smell, that was the most painful part of Guatemala.

By December, Marilyn got very homesick for her friends and family and decided she was going home. We had planned to stay until March, and I was very depressed even though I knew Marilyn was not that happy, I did not want her to leave. After she joyfully left, I came down with a flu and on Christmas Eve, I was standing in the airport waiting to get on a plane as I knew Christmas day there would be a seat. I was also homesick, I love celebrating Christmas with my family and even though I arrived in the evening I was at least home and I got over my flu immediately. I returned to my classes in Spanish and Art in January and continued studying Spanish hoping to continue traveling in South America.

I was ending my dysfunctional relationship with Marilyn and felt even more abandoned by her when I asked if I could visit her and she said no. I knew then that she really could not be there for me because of her poor health and knew I needed to meet someone more available.

A year later, in 1994, Josefina entered my life again. My dear friends Ruthie and Judy made it happen. I went over to where Josefina was staying and she was crying because her girlfriend had dropped her. I could not deal with her pain so thank goodness I could offer her my Buddhist practice and she began to chant. Josefina started interviewing me with her tape recorder as that is what she did in Mexico working for a TV station. After a while we became lovers and as usual it was difficult because I really cannot live with anyone and she wanted to have a live-in relationship. She then found a great place to live, we began a long relationship and when I asked what she thought a relationship was, she said, "A relationship is a long conversation." I did not like that, though now after 20 years, I understand what she meant as we usually talk everyday.

Chapter 37, Ecuador

In December 1993, after Roxanne's passing, I decided I wanted to go to Ecuador as I met someone who told me it had wonderful Spanish schools for foreigners. I went to the Ecuadorian Embassy and the man there said immediately, "Go to Alvarado Travel Agency and ask for the owner Mr. Alvarado," which I did. When I went there Mr. Alvarado—or Juan—seemed to be too aristocratic to be working in a travel agency. When I told him I was looking for a home I might stay in for a month, he said to me without hesitation, "Go and stay with Yolanda my wife." She was in Quito, the capital of Ecuador. I was surprised he did not even ask me any questions but I was to learn later why he was anxious for me to stay with his wife.

When the plane landed in Quito and I exited the airport, I was amazed to see my name in big letters on a poster. Two lovely wealthy people greeted me, one was Mr. Alvarado's son, Juan, and the other was his wife, Ana. They rushed me away to their big Cadillac. I knew I was in for a surprise and sure enough I was. When we arrived at the elegant grand house that had broken bottles placed upside down to keep thieves out, Mrs. Alvarado was happy to meet me and immediately after her son left she started to ask me about her husband, how he looked, how he was, I could not believe how she immediately opened up her entire life to me, a total stranger. I was later to learn her father had been president of Ecuador and had died in a plane crash. Juan, her husband, had been president of the Ecuador airlines, and had gotten involved with a crook from Argentina. When Juan was to be arrested, he fled the country to San Francisco. He married an American to be able to stay in the U.S. Yolanda did not want to go to the States as she did not want to leave her country, coming from such a well known family. What she told me next was even more shocking. This handsome crook from Argentina, whom nobody had ever seen up until then, then began to court their daughter, Sofia. Sofia dated him for a year and then they were to get married. Mr. Alvarado hired a private plane to come home to Quito, so he could walk his daughter down the aisle to the alter.

When the Argentinian heard Mr. Alvarado was returning to Quito, he fled. Now Yolanda had a second horrible scandal which was in all the local newspapers. Sofia fled to Florida and opened up her own travel agency, she was so humiliated. Yolanda was left all alone in this big house, all her family lived in the U.S., except for her son Juan. She told me she could not leave Quito because her whole life had been there and now her son and his two children were her whole life. Yolanda spoke perfect English and after that evening she said, "From now on we only speak Spanish." Her servant fed me and I visited her for one hour of Spanish, which I did not enjoy so I soon found a school I attended every day for five hours.

I was robbed once in the market as I took out my wallet from my pocket, a man ran by me and grabbed the wallet and fled. Thank goodness I only had lost ten dollars. I had been warned by many people that there were many thieves in Quito. I had been told so I was not that shocked. Walking home took two hours, but I was able to observe the beauty of Quito which stands high in the Andes, the snow-capped mountains surrounding the city with a breathtaking view against the striking clear-blue skies. Clouds covered part of the top of the mountains. I became so mesmerized by the beauty that I forgot about the robbery.

One weekend my teacher, Rose, took me to her town. We traveled sitting on top of the train which was free, with many other people.

I find most Latinos very friendly but Yolanda was not that friendly—she was too miserable except when her grandchildren stayed with her on the weekend. She was in heaven, laughing and playing with them. Some nights I would hear her crying. Only once did she invite me to watch a telenovela with her, but otherwise she stayed by herself. Yolanda called her husband every Sunday night and they talked for quite a while. She hated her son Juan's wife calling her *la bruja*, the witch.

Her friends visited her to play cards each week, they wanted to talk to me but she did not permit this. I was to eat my meals alone in the kitchen with the servant. I was grieving Roxanne's passing so I just kept studying my Spanish for the month I spent in Quito. It was an interesting experience but I was happy to return home. I realized Mr. Alvarado loved Yolanda but had to stay in the U.S. When I returned home I became aware that I had been a part of a crucial moment in the life of a prominent figure in Ecuadorian history.

Chapter 38, Highlights of My Trip to Spain

September to December 1997

I wanted to learn Spanish and found a wonderful teacher named Mr. Jordan. After taking his Spanish class for 5 years, which covered the language and the culture of Spain, I decided to go to Spain and live for two months and then travel for one month with my friend Josefina who would join me in November.

I arrived in Madrid on September 2nd to a huge, crowded, gorgeous city. It was extremely hot. Immediately, I found the Spanish people to be very strong, loud, and aggressive. Even with my 5 years of studying Spanish, I felt alone and vulnerable. I had enough courage to speak and ask directions, which made me very happy. I found a hotel in the center of the city and climbed up the thirty five steps to my room.

I did not feel comfortable in Madrid, as there were too many people rushing, but I wanted to go to the Prado Museum. I couldn't wait to see the famous Spanish painters, Velazquez and Goya. Mr. Jordan had mentioned that Velazquez had been one of the greatest artists in the world but had not been acknowledged by most art historians. Goya was one of the first artists to paint emotions and the suffering of poor people. It was fascinating, I spent the entire day in the museum and met an art historian who showed me writings on Velasquez's paintings which were in Hebrew, proving he was Jewish. I knew the Spanish Inquisition had been horrible so to find out Velasquez was Jewish and that it had not been revealed amazed me. The buildings in Madrid were beautiful with many different kinds of architecture; Gothic, Renaissance, and Romanesque dominated the center of the city.

The day after I went to the museum, I left for Salamanca where I was to study Spanish for two months. The three-hour bus ride took us through very dry, arid country. I can only remember seeing signs with pictures of bulls as we passed through the countryside where these animals are raised for bullfights. When I arrived in Salamanca, it was very hot and crowded with many tourists and students.

Salamanca is well known for its university which is the second oldest in Europe. Many festivals are held in September and I found the city so overwhelming with all the people trying to enjoy the last days of their vacations. I decided to go to Galicia, it has a great forest and the famous cathedral Santiago de Compostela, which houses the remains of Jesus's apostle St. James, and contains the largest incense burner in the world. It fills the room with the the aroma of incense as it continuously swings back and forth, which had a mesmerizing effect on me. This is also where the famous pilgrimage from France to Galicia ends after people have walked hundreds of miles as a spiritual experience. I saw many nuns in their long, black habits arriving from that pilgrimage. I could not believe they had walked that distance in such clothing.

After one day there, I realized I was so close to Portugal I could catch a bus and visit another country. Immediately, I felt a huge difference upon arriving to Portugal. The people were warm and friendly, and the food was a lot tastier to me. Portugal has rich soil so it grows more vegetables. Spanish food is mostly meat and starches, as the land is arid and dry. I wished I could have stayed and studied Spanish in Portugal, but that was impossible. While I was there, I visited Porto, the wine capital of Portugal. It was located on a river that had boats and looked like the Italian gondolas in Venice, Italy. Though I had ten years of sobriety, I gave it up in Porto because the wine was so delicious. I thought, I had learned to drink in moderation, but once again I became an alcoholic, for ten years. Living in denial was a common form of my existence my entire life.

Most of the houses in Portugal are covered with colorful tiles. They are all works of art, especially in Lisbon where the city is like a museum. Pictures of flowers and historical events were painted on those tiles which are outstandingly colorful.

I stayed in Portugal for a week then headed back to Salamanca, as I had to enroll in my school to study Spanish. The school provided a host family for my lodging and food. I chose the school "Miguel de Unamuno," named for a famous president of the University of Salamanca. He had been a great revolutionary against the royalty in the 1800s because of the huge amount of poverty in Spain.

I liked my host family immediately. Their handsome teenage boys were both studying English, and I was able to have a daily Spanish-English exchange with them. We had a great time as they were both fun-loving kids who never stopped entertaining us with their adventures in school and their holidays in different parts of Spain.

At night, their mother, Carmen, would cook wonderful meals for all of us and also played the guitar while we sang Spanish folk songs. There were two other students staying in Carmen's big home.

I had the smallest room—8 by 10 feet—because I wanted the convenience of being near the bathroom.

On the weekends, I traveled to many historical sites. I visited the small town of Alba, which is about two hours away from Salamanca. The ancient houses in Alba were built out of dirt and wood. The first floor was for the animals, the second for grain and other food, while the people lived on the third floor, the top floor.

On another weekend I went to Avila where St. Teresa had been in prison most of her life for standing up against the leaders of the country when they tried to kill all the Jewish people. It was part of the Inquisition, a 700-year "cleansing" of Arabs, Muslims, and Jews in Spain.

After I returned from Avila, I had a dream I was part of the Inquisition as a killer of the Jewish people. Many years later, after I'd been hurt in relationships with numerous Jewish people, I saw my karma and realized why that might have had happened. What goes around comes around, maybe I had been one of those assassins in a past life?

Amazingly, when I was 7 years old, I had chosen the name Theresa for my first communion. I chose the name out of nowhere. It came out my imagination, and where does our imagination come from? My dream and my unconscious connection to St. Theresa had helped me understand my karma with Jewish people.

After two months of studying and traveling on the weekends, Josefina arrived November 1ˢᵗ. It was good to see her as I really wanted to travel all over Spain and she was the perfect companion. She wanted to visit the town of Caparroso, where her grandfather and his family had lived. They had come from Italy and all had red hair. The Spanish citizens had black hair, so the Caparroso stood out, and for that the town was named after them.

Our first journey together was going south through dry, arid desert country as we headed for Andalucía, where the famous Flamenco was created. I was excited to see this part of Spain; it definitely was the most alive and colorful area. Women wore vibrant clothes, and the people were more friendly than in the north. Music was constantly heard coming out of people's homes and the many cafes. The food in Andalucía had more of the Arabic influence, with a wonderful variety of spices. On our second night there, we went to a Flamenco show, which we loved. The people from Andalucía have been greatly influenced by the gypsies called *gitanos* whose origin is from the Arab world. I had my palm read and bought jewelry from the wonderful gypsies. They live in their horse-drawn wagons and travel all over Spain in their caravans.

Next, we headed for Cordoba to see the most famous Mezquita (Mosque) in Spain. This Mezquita was huge, and we easily got lost because it was so enormous. The bright, beautiful colors of red and yellow on the stone arches still remained after hundreds of years. The mosque was built on the base of the San Vicente Martir Basilique, which was shared both by the Muslims and Christians until recent times. I saw many statues of famous men who all looked Jewish with their long Sephardic noses. In these statues I could see how important the Jews were in Spain. They covered up their identity by converting to Catholicism because they did not want to be discovered as Jews and be slaughtered. Queen Isabella and her husband Fernando were responsible for this horror. They have a museum in Madrid which has all the structures that were used in the inquisition to kill and torture Jews, Arabs, and Muslims. I could not visit such a torture chamber that had been created by such evil people.

When we visited Andalucía, I was in awe of its vibrancy. The beautiful gardens there have many varieties of flowers from different countries. The colors and arrangements were unique with a variety of angles and shapes. We loved the architecture, too, with its many fountains. The gardens and buildings are small, both from the time of the Arabs before the Christian invasion, which began the horrible "cleansing."

Our next stop was the fabulous city of Granada, with the incredible Alhambra, which is another wonder of the world. The embroidery-like architecture with its twists and turns are something one must see, it is so awesome. It too, had many fountains and gardens. It also had towers from which we could see the entire city. There were also structures that were small and felt almost like children play houses. The people of that time must have been quite small.

Barcelona, another wonder of the world, was our next stop. I have never seen architecture like Barcelona's. It looked as if everything was made out of pottery. Gaudi, the famous Barcelona architect, came from a family of potters. The huge church he began building in the early 1900s is still not finished to this day. Even so, it is also considered to be one of the wonders of the world. Most of the architecture in Barcelona has been influenced by Gaudi. We visited his home there with its amazing architecture, including the gardens full of mosaic flower structures. He built his own furniture, and his bed was quite tiny. He must have been a very short man, as everything in his little home was small.

We went to a concert one night. I don't remember anything about the music, but the people were so noisy during the intermission I could not believe it. I vividly recall the entire interior which was totally full of green and white mosaic structures like flowers and other ornate pottery designs. The influence of Gaudi is felt everywhere in Barcelona.

Next we headed for Pamplona, where the bulls run in the streets once a year and all the tourists are chased by them. This did not happen when we were there, thank goodness! It was not that interesting of a city so we left and continued our journey back to Madrid.

During our travels in Spain, Josefina and I really enjoyed going to the museums and the different inexpensive restaurants where we could watch the daily soccer games on the television. All the cathedrals in Europe are freezing in the winter because they have no heat, so it is amazing that no matter how cold, people visit them and the devoted Catholic women in black sit there for hours with their rosary beads in their freezing hands.

Josefina and I got along quite well except when she took an entire day to shop for a pair of shoes. It was freezing and rainy the last few weeks. After three memorable months, I felt very fortunate to have had this great experience, yet happy to be going home for the holidays.

Chapter 39, December 2002: Australia

When I heard that the Gay Olympics were going to be held in Sydney, Australia in December of 2002 and that there was going to be a swim event for Seniors, I immediately wanted to go and compete. I was 66 years-old and had all the requirements to sign up through the internet for the 100-yard freestyle.

I was surprised that on my departure date and entering a United Airlines flight, I was on a plane packed with gay people, mostly men. I was totally exhausted when we arrived 18 hours later to Sydney, since most of the flight time was spent talking with different groups of gay and lesbian people. Upon arrival I made several calls to different hotels but finally found a youth hostel as that was all I could afford. It really was the best choice, since from all my traveling around the world, I found that youth hostels were always filled with wonderful and friendly people and more so, because this event included gay people from all over the world. As it was customary from my other travels, I chose to sleep on the top of a bunk bed because I hate to be awaken by someone who is sleeping above me.

When I went to the Olympic Village, I could not believe there were hundreds of gays and lesbians from all over the United States, Japan and Europe. I saw a few from San Francisco and we hung out for a while but I liked exploring Sydney alone, as the city has an abundance of museums and art galleries.

I soon learned that Sydney was not affected by the AIDS epidemic of the late 80s and is something you can observe by the three different areas specifically populated by gay and lesbian people. I had never seen so many gay men in one place. It made me realized how horrible the U.S. had been affected by AIDS, especially in San Francisco.

I signed up for the 100-yard swim event and when I went to the main pool to compete, I found out there were no other women. I was very sad to learn this since this event was the main reason why I made this trip. The organizers told me that, "For one hundred dollars I could have a first place gold medal," I immediately said, "No thank you." That was the end of my sport activities at the Sydney Gay Olympic Games.

I decided I to explore the city since it was so rich in culture, arts and activities. I noticed through the gay newspapers that there were theatre plays and performances in the evenings, most of them concerned with many gay issues from different places around the world. Visiting the museums in Sydney was very interesting, not only for what they showed but also because in every one of them, the Aborigines people were the main workers. They were in charge of taking people on tours, selling things at the book stores and also giving lectures on history and geography of the country. It appeared to me that there was a sort of underlying guilty feeling coming from the white Australian population for all the horrible treatment inflicted upon the Aborigines by the White Man.

The city of Sydney is quite beautiful, reminding me of England with a huge amount of parks, where rich green grass and a myriad of flowers grow despite Australia suffering from a drought every year. I was informed that there is an abundance of underground water. I became aware of the beauty and was fascinated with a museum that had nothing but installations, which are large spaces filled with different pieces made out of cloth, wood, or steel and of every shape and color. I must have stayed in that museum for hours, as each of the installations I observed was unique and stood out in space and stimulated my imagination more than any painting. It reminded me of the installation I had made in an art class I had taken in Santa Rosa City College, just after the 9-11 bombing happened in New York. I created an installation simulating five towers made out of 4 x 9 sheets of plastic, these were twisted in circles and they had multiple lights shining underneath, giving the effect of enlightenment after a disaster. I won first place in the event.

Another fantastic experience was going to the Sydney Symphony Hall which has a very interesting architecture made out of a multitude of shapes and forms of wood. This music hall is one of the most important emblems from the city and appears in almost all the tourist guides of Sydney. I had never heard the sound of music like angels and horns were vibrating sent from the heavens like it did in there, it gave me goose bumps as I listened to Beethoven's 9th Symphony.

Then I heard about the Outback, the part of the country where the Aborigines originated. I decided I must go. I flew on a small plane. I had been told that in the Outback, people have experienced dreams of loved ones who had passed on and I wanted to have a dream of my daughter Roxanne because I never had one since her passing. Fortunately, on the second night of being in the Outback, I had a wonderful experience. Before seeing her, I heard her loud and strong laughter, then immediately I saw her alongside me on a beach somewhere in South America. We were running, laughing and having a lovely intimate time. I could see her beautiful brown eyes with her bright smile and when I woke up, I was full of gratitude and peace, especially because never before had I dreamed of her until that awesome night.

The Outback land is a place one must see, as each day at dusk everyone can observe different shades of red, yellow, or blue in the desert. The land stores food in the ground that only the Aborigines know about. Most of the food is dug out and consists of grains and seeds—this is why Western food is needed to be flown in daily for the many tourists who visit there. We stayed in cabins that had a tent top; you could hear the sound of the wind and other elements in the wide open magnificent space. The next day I went on a dream walk, which was suggested and which consisted of a guide taking us in a two hour walk through the desert, where I relived my dream with Roxanne. We walked through winding mountains of desert, lost in conversation with my beloved child. I was in a trance for days after that powerful experience.

Later I saw a movie about the Aborigines and their intense connection with the people who have passed on, and how they have received messages from the dead on how to survive.

The Aborigines paint their dark faces with white chalk and do their ceremonies walking in a circle while chanting sounds which are mesmerizing and hypnotic, over and over again for hours. Maybe all these rituals and ceremonies are one of the many reasons why they have survived for many centuries, besides the fact that they don't have interracial marriages.

I had gone to Australia for the Gay Olympic Games, but what I found was an incredible impression left in my heart by my dream experience with the Aborigines and their culture. The memory and the experience of the Outback, with its flat land and the people living in caves and where one cannot see any vegetation, will never leave me.

Chapter 40, Cuba

My First Cuban Experience: 2003

With a badly sprained ankle, I went to Cuba with Josefina. It was January 3rd, 2003, and it was my 67th birthday. I had always wanted to go to Cuba and now I was going, even with a walking cast. Nothing could stop me. We wanted to have an authentic Cuban experience, and we were going to stay with a Cuban family. We stayed with Grecia, who was a Professor of Chemistry at the University of Havana; she lived with her boyfriend and her 23 year old son, Ahmed. Ahmed greeted us at the airport with big hugs and kisses. The airport felt like an old fifties movie. Everything there was from the early fifties, before the Revolution: the chairs, tables, and all the benches were made out of oak. I felt like I had gone back in time where people dressed simply in their cotton clothes, there was such warmth in the weather and the people.

We waited in the inspection line quite some time, not wanting a Cuban stamp on our passport as it was unacceptable on our return to the U.S. When we left the airport, old cars were everywhere, and huge billboard signs supporting the revolution appeared along the road to our destination. I said to Josefina "I can see Castro coming down these roads as I had watched him enter Havana in 1950 on my television."

Ahmed was as most of the youth—they do not want to live in Cuba. They want to come to the U.S. so they can buy the material possessions they see on television. Since 1994, when Cubans in Miami were allowed to visit their families, they brought with them all kinds of commercial goods. This merchandise infected the country with dollars and forced Fidel Castro to open up dollar stores. Many Cubans live off dollars coming from relatives who live in the U.S. The presence of the black market was everywhere. A man came to Grecia's home and took out cheese and chickens from his backpack to sell to us.

It was not cheap to live in this home. Food was scarce and very expensive. However, we wanted to have a Cuban home experience, and that we did, night and day.

We were shocked by the bed we were given to sleep in. It had springs jutting up and out from the mattress, and this was the best bed in the house. We somehow learned to find the in-between spaces to survive. It was very cold at night, and Josefina said, "I am going to cover myself with papers and plastic like the poor people do in

Mexico," while I put all my clothes from my suitcase over the thin cotton wool sheet that was given us. The next day we bought a new blanket.

The bathroom facilities were sparse. We had to pour water down the toilet to flush the waste material. We boiled cold water every morning to take our shower, pouring small buckets of hot water over our freezing body.

The family was warm and loving. We felt at home, and I was never ungrateful for this experience. Because food was so scarce, one person was given monthly rations: six pounds of rice, six pounds of beans, one pound of sugar, a half liter of oil, one bar of soap, toothpaste, one chicken, six eggs, two pounds of delicious powdered milk, two pounds of spaghetti, and one pack of hot dogs. Everyone went to the local store early in the morning to get their huge piece of Castro bread. Their rent, electricity, and water were paid for by the Government. The city plumbing was bad, running water was not regular. Because of the poor living conditions, there was no incentive for the youth to work even though we saw many billboards encouraging people to appreciate their work and to continue to fight for the Revolution. Castro was the Big Papa who appeared on the non-commercial television regularly to talk to the people. I noticed he had a nervous twitch and talked for long periods of time.

Eating became a big event in the house because of our bringing dollars. We would go to the dollar store daily and stand in long lines to buy food from the U.S. at a very high price. Ahmed was so happy because we had enough money to buy extra food for them that we take for granted as Americans. Ahmed would say at every meal, "I love *carne*." He eventually did come to the U.S.

The family lived like kings for the eight days we stayed there. They would invite neighbors who were delighted at the rare feast we offered. These meals each day were like parties. Everyone was so happy, and I always thought about how spoiled we are in the United States.

Public transportation was another big challenge because of the extremely crowded buses. Chino, our hosts' neighbor, would take us to the center each day for two dollars in his old 1950 Chevrolet.

I observed Cubans to be extremely strong and very lively people. Music is heard on every block as musicians come from all over the world to play with the local artists. The Cubans are incredible athletes and usually always win the Pan American games. I have never seen such wonderful, alive, healthy kids; they love school as there are many available adults who love to help them. Mulattos are the dominant race and are so beautiful to look at, with their soft brown skin and shining eyes full of life.

Grecia had pictures all over her bedroom of her husband Cesar who left her to live in the U.S. I asked, "Does this bother your boyfriend?" She responded, "No he knows I will always love Cesar." Ahmed was so handsome and looked just like his father, whom he adored. Cesar married a woman in Miami so he could stay in the the US. I recently heard that he was in an accident and had a big financial settlement, and he moved back to Havana to be with Grecia.

My Second Trip to Cuba June 2003

This time that I went to Cuba, I went with Global Exchange, an educational group, for 12 days. I wanted to see how this country works from the inside as we were taken on many excursions sponsored by the Government. We went to see a huge city garden where all the neighbors plant organic vegetables which later are sold to the people.

I could not get over how proud the people were of their country, it was just the opposite of what I had heard on television in the States. The people loved their country with a passion and they wanted to celebrate every event related to the Revolution.

We were taken to a huge modern government building where a man educated us on how the Cubans survive with very little gasoline. The embargo the U.S. has put on the Cubans has not stopped them from being extremely creative. They use batteries for energy and have created huge transformers to generate this energy.

What impressed me was how many people could fit into a car built in the 1950s, which are quite large. They are used as taxis, four people in the front seat and five in the back. Everyone seemed to have a wonderful sense of humor and I never saw many angry people like you see in the U.S. The government takes care of its people and you feel it. There are no people with fancy clothes, everyone dresses very plain, but they are a happy people. I never saw a police man, the people love their country.

Our guide from Global Exchange was an American woman who was married to a Cuban man, she was pregnant and very happy to show us her country as she called Cuba "my country." Marriage is not common in Cuba—people live together as long as they get along. There is no forced living together as the government supplies housing. You live with people you feel comfortable with. I saw five older women living together happily not having to worry about family taking care of them.

Che Guevara is adored even more than Castro, he is an icon and you see more pictures of him than Castro. Castro adored him and always referred to him in his daily talks on T.V. No one listened to Castro as they said, "He talks too much."

The sounds of music are everywhere in Cuba. It is a country where musicians can play everyday if they want to, and they do. They do not have to worry about their survival. I think that is why they are such a happy people. Also they are always talking with each other. We walked from La Havana to a town where hundreds of people gathered in a beautiful resort place to celebrate World Peace. We walked through the mountains where Castro and his army had hidden before the Revolution broke out. This gave us a glimpse on how Castro and his army had survived while living in caves in the mountains.

Another important event was seeing the Cuban Ballet where all the men and women were very small but amazingly talented, moving with incredible speed. I went backstage after the performance as we were welcomed to visit with the dancers. Many dancers do leave Cuba and go to other countries as they want more money and freedom of expression in their dancing and choreographing.

We also visited several schools where we saw many teachers and assistants helping small groups of children. Since I have been a teacher, I know the value of education. I could not get over how healthy and alive the Cuban youth were, they were full of life and expressed themselves so well. Communication is so important in Cuba, the youth had no shyness, they were encouraged to express themselves and that they did very well. They were full of questions for our group as they wanted to know who we were and why we were in Cuba.

My Third Trip to Cuba

On my third visit of that same year, 2003, I went alone as I wanted to travel with my friend Grecia. We were headed for Santiago, which is supposed to have the best music in Cuba. We were traveling by bus as I love to talk to people on my trips around the world.

On our first night we stopped in Santa Clara, a hundred miles from La Havana. This is where Che Guevara began the march for the Revolution, a historical site. There is a huge train boxcar on the side of the tracks where all the ammunition was stored for the march into Havana at the beginning of the Revolution in 1950. I remember watching it on TV.

On our first night out, we went to a nightclub to dance. I decided to put all my money in the front pocket of my jeans, which totaled $700. When I went up to the bar to buy us some drinks, three very handsome men surrounded me dancing, laughing, and joking. The music was blasting and everybody was happy having a great time. When I put my hand in my pocket to pay for drinks I could not believe my money was not there, it was gone. Somehow they had robbed me, putting their hands in my pocket and I never felt it.

It was a horrible and frightening experience since there is no way to get money in Cuba because there are no ATM machines. Fortunately, we had already paid for one night where we were staying, but the next day we had to get back to La Havana and we had no money. Luckily, Grecia found a friend who took us back.

I became so ill and frightened that Grecia took me to the doctor. I was seen immediately and given medicine freely. I had never had such a sensitive, caring doctor before. I really appreciated how great the medical system is in Cuba. I can see why they send more doctors out into the world than any other country. They are experts in all fields of medicine and have discovered amazing treatments and cures for cancer and many other diseases.

After a week of recovering I had to come back to the U.S., but I didn't have money to leave the country as one needs to pay a hundred dollar airport tax. I called my daughter everyday so she could send me money but it was impossible to have a conversation with her. The phone lines were extremely old, but she managed to understand I had no money. Then my niece heard about what had happened and she told me that a friend who was a musician from San Francisco was coming to Cuba to buy a guitar and would bring me money so I could leave the country!

I was never so grateful as I was at that moment for such a miracle.

While I was waiting for this young man to come, Grecia told me of her life with her husband Cesar. She said that men have sex with other women and it is accepted. What I found weird was Ahmed told me how his father had taught him to have sex with animals, that was hard for me to hear. Cubans have such sexual energy, you can feel it in the air. Sex is everywhere; they take full advantage of it.

Chapter 41, 2006

Since I was now retired, I could go to South America any time. My two good Buddhist friends, Chico and Josefina, wanted to go with me, which made me happy. Since they are both Buddhist, we were going to visit the many Buddhist centers in South America. Although I had been studying Spanish, I could not speak to people that well but my two companions spoke perfect Spanish.

Josefina, Chico, and I left San Francisco on December 8, 2005. When we arrived in São Paulo, the largest city in Brazil, it was a dream come true for me. On our first night we stayed at the Ikeda hotel, which amazed us as Ikeda is the name of our Buddhist mentor. The hotel was near the huge SGI Buddhist Culture Center.

We were so excited to be in Brazil that we could not sleep, especially Josefina. At the hostel we stayed in, there were only two beds so Josefina chose to sleep on a table with a blanket underneath her body.

Hotels in Brazil were clean and inexpensive, and they always offered free breakfast with the night stay. Breakfast was awesome: hard boiled eggs, many different kinds of fruit, wonderful fresh rolls, and of course, great coffee.

As the Buddhist Culture Center was only a few blocks away, we literally ran to it after our first breakfast in Brazil. The Japanese members there were more alive and friendly than Japanese people I'd met in other parts of the world. There are more SGI Buddhists in São Paulo than any other place in the world besides Japan. We were fortunate to be there when they were having a big annual culture festival. The Japanese members—young and old—danced freely like the Brazilian members. It was a two-day festival, and we were treated like royalty. They could not do enough for us.

We had our own personal guide who showed us the many interesting sites of the city. An enormous amount of Japanese people had immigrated to Brazil after World War II, and they had a large Japantown in São Paulo, called Liberdade. We went there after we left the Buddhist center, and walked into another celebration. There was live music everywhere and plenty of booths with Japanese food. We enjoyed the entertainment while we ate our fill of delicious sushi and tamari chicken.

Brazil has to have the best cuisine in South America. I never had a bad meal there. The restaurants served food buffet-style with enormous choices. It was also a country with healthier land than any other country on that continent. Fruits and vegetables were delicious and cheap. We could not get over having so much healthy food at a very low price.

Curitiba, the cultural capital of Brazil, was our next stop. The Oscar Niemeyer museum had the most outrageous ultra modern architecture I had ever seen. There were huge, expansive spaces that made me feel that I was part of a gigantic cosmos. The museum was filled with paintings of Brazilian artists from past and present.

Next we visited the world famous Iguaçu Waterfalls. The biggest ones in the world, they extend for a mile from Brazil into Argentina. Standing under the falls, I felt the incredible power of water. To get there, we took an overnight bus ride, passing many coffee plantations on the way. Brazil has the most comfortable buses I ever experienced. I actually slept on these buses, the seats turn into comfortable beds, which I had never seen before.

I did not feel Brazil was a poor country until we got to Rio de Janeiro. Here, in this famous city of beaches and beauty, drugs and poverty prevailed. At the same time, Rio was such an alive city. It seemed that everyone was dancing, and the women wore bikinis that showed how gorgeous they kept their bodies.

The people in Rio were warm and friendly and were all trying to talk with us everywhere we went. They were curious about North America and wanted to know why we came to Brazil. Most of them wanted to go to the U.S. They wanted to experience what they saw on television.

While we were in Rio, we climbed to the top of a mountain where a huge statue of Jesus stands. The statue felt like it was at least a mile high. I could not bend my head far enough back to see his face. Everybody there was praying out loud and screaming "Jesus!" along with all their requests for His help. As we were not Christians, we simply enjoyed being thousands of feet high and seeing Rio below with the lovely blue sea shining brilliantly in the sun.

Our next stop was Uruguay, a very modern, beautiful country. There was not that much poverty as the government had taken care of its people since the revolution in 1980. I did not like the food, which tasted like most fast food in America. There was no native cooking due to the lack of indigenous people in the area. They had fled to Paraguay or had been killed when the Europeans came and conquered South America.

We were in Uruguay only two days and then took a bus boat to Argentina. I was horrified to see that all the water was brown and terribly dirty. We bought many gifts on the boat as there was no tax, and they had a wonderful collection of blankets, clothes, jewelry, and crockery that indigenous people from many countries in South America had made.

When we arrived in Buenos Aires, the capital city of Argentina, I felt like we were in Italy. The people spoke Spanish combined with many Italian words. They also had the same humor and warmth the Italians have. We were excited to be in the biggest city in South America. All the architecture looked just like that of Rome or Paris. It was built by Europeans like most of the cities in South America.

My friend Chico's big thrill was going to gay bars and picking up men. We had made a rule that he could not bring home any men, and he was very good about it. Josefina and I were shocked though, as at a museum Chico hit on one of the workers and went into the bathroom with him. They did their thing there, and then separated. Gay men are so different from gay women. Many of them just want to get connected for a few minutes of sex, and that is it.

While we were in Buenos Aires, we went to see the tango. There were only old people there, but I did not mind. It was amazing to see elderly people dancing for long periods of time and not tiring. I tried to dance, and it was not easy. The tango is not a difficult dance, but the men must lead you. I had a hard time following the gentleman who had invited me to dance. I guess the tango will soon die if there are no youth to carry on the famous Argentinian tradition of dance.

Beef is the main food in Argentina, and you see people eating it for breakfast, lunch, and dinner. Fruits and vegetables are rare as the country does not have much good soil for raising produce. Beef and delicious bread and pastries and are the main foods along with wonderful rich, yogurt and other milk products. These were all affordable and plentiful.

Next we headed to Cordoba, where Che Guevara was born. We went to the museum dedicated to him, and it was educational and interesting. We learned that Che had studied to be a doctor. He might have been motivated to learn about medicine because he had been sick his whole life with asthma.

The museum in Buenos Aires dedicated to "Evita" was also incredibly interesting as I knew about her only through the famous film on her. She was loved and adored in Argentina as it showed in the museum with the many pictures of her life. She came from poverty and never forgot it. She gave generously to the poor when she was married to Peron who was the dictator in the 1950s.

We then headed for Chile. Josefina knew a great deal of South American history, so she was always telling me stories of different writers and politicians in South America. She told me about the 60s when the military police shot Salvador Allende. When we went into his home in Santiago, however, the guard lied and said he died a natural death. We realized then the history of Chile was changed there to hide the truth. Pinochet, the horrible dictator, was revered there.

I had a dear friend, Monica, whose Chilean family was very rich. She would tell me how great Pinochet was. When I disagreed with her, she showed me papers of how the people loved him. I knew it was propaganda. A year ago, my friend Monica committed suicide. I always wondered if finding out the truth had some part in driving her to take her own life.

The food in Chile was not that good. I figured they shipped all their great vegetables and fruits to other countries. I was glad to leave and continue my travels.

Going next to Bolivia, my friends and I were anxious to see La Paz, the highest city in the world. The altitude in Bolivia makes it difficult for tourists to survive for more than a few hours. Because I am a swimmer and have strong lungs, I had no problem with the high altitude. Chico and Josefina were both ill though, and had to chew coca leaves to survive. We stayed 5 days in the hotel in order for them to stay in bed to recuperate.

The food in Bolivia was not that good at all either and I was anxious to leave. The only thing that interested me in that city, besides getting stoned on coca leaves, was seeing all the women wearing the famous English round bowler hats with colorful skirts and shoes that looked like they were for men.

One of the unexpected highlights of our trip was crossing through the Andes from Chile to Peru. The winding road on that unexpected, exciting day, was stunning because of the height and the views of the snow-capped mountains.

I was dying to go to Machu Picchu, the ancient Inca city built in the mountains of Peru 7,970 feet above sea level. My friends were getting used to the high altitudes, and we had coca leaves to chew on whenever it bothered us.

As we took the train ride there, I was screaming with excitement. The high altitude and the energy there is a high in itself.

It too, is a wonder of the world, and it is sad that soon it will be closed to the public because tourists are ruining the place by chipping off pieces of the rocks for souvenirs.

At the end of our trip, we visited friends of my niece Lorraine. The mother greeted us carrying a picture of my niece who lived in Lima, Peru. I could not get over their generosity and hospitality. Awesome food was prepared by their indigenous cook who made dishes from her culture.

Josefina, Chico, and I flew home to San Francisco with great happiness after having a most enjoyable time. It was quite amazing how well we got along for the 5 weeks we had traveled together. It was January, 2006—a new year. We were amazed how fast the 5 weeks of travel had passed.

Chapter 42, South Africa 2010

Ruth Levy, my dear friend from South Africa had raved about her country for years. She was born in Cape Town during the terrible time of apartheid. Her parents had fled Nazi Germany after their entire family had been sent to the ovens in Dachau. They cried every day over their loss and outside Germany, Ruth was to see the horror of the Africanos treating the black man with such savagery. She had constant nightmares and grew up an extremely frightened, but a kind woman whom everyone loves.

This was to be my final long distance trip of my life, traveling around the world to South Africa on December 3, 2010. I had saved enough miles to travel free. I left San Francisco at two in the afternoon and six hours later I arrived in New York where I was to wait an entire cold exhausting length of time to catch my connecting flight to Johannesburg. On the plane to South Africa I was to sit next to a kind gentleman of color from Cape Town. We talked for many hours of how his country had changed but racism was still very painful. The youth had overcome the history of racism as they had not the background of the brutality of the White Man as he had experienced.

I was very excited, and even though I was alone, I felt confident as there were practicing Buddhists in Johannesburg and Cape Town so I knew I would have a human connection one way or another. I checked into a hostel in the outskirts of Johannesburg which was huge and full of friendly foreigners that made me feel good. Being very trustworthy, I did not lock up my belongings and when I returned that night I found many of my things missing. Never having had that experience before, I soon found out the world had changed since I began hosteling in 1962.

I did not feel comfortable traveling in the big city but I immediately saw a pronounced difference between the black people in Africa and the black people in the U.S.: the Africanos, as they are called, were not as confident or outgoing as the American black people. I felt them more submissive there. That was not to be for the younger generation, they have the confidence as they were not subjugated to the horrors of the White Man as their parents had suffered. Sadly, I did find our Buddhist community center but it was closed tight with no sign of when there might be a gathering. I felt upset as I had always found our SGI community centers opened in other parts of the world.

I decided after returning to the hostel and noticing some of my clothes missing to leave the next day for Cape Town where I had phone numbers of SGI members. It was a short three hour flight. When I arrived I felt at home with the lovely Table Mountains surrounding the city and the gorgeous Atlantic and Indian Oceans merging right in front of my eyes. I could not wait to go to the Cape of Good Hope where I was to put one foot in the cold Atlantic and the other foot in the warm Indian Ocean at same time; that was to be one of the most awesome moments of my life especially since being in water has always been one of my greatest passions.

The youth hostel was wonderful with a gay woman at the desk greeting me. We became friends immediately and I enjoyed talking to her daily. She was an interesting woman who guided me daily on where to go in the city. Cape Town is a walking city as it is small and the White Man has created many fascinating places to visit such as the Jewish museum which was built by the German Jews who fled from Hitler's Holocaust.

The huge Table Mountains protect this small city like a cape and that is why it is called Cape Town. Never had I been in a place that has so much natural beauty but the White Man who came here caused such pain for the Black Man. The Black Man created a museum in a big old house in an historically black area. In this house, photos and movies show the brutality of the White Man towards the Black population. I remember the black woman who greeted me at the museum, she was friendly but I could feel her anger as she had endured much of what was shown in the photos and the movies that I watched for the two hours I spent there. My friend Ruthie who had grown up in Cape Town had shared many of these horrifying stories of the city with me. The brutality was unimaginably cruel as the White Man could treat his slave any way he chose, beating them with whips and belts until they bled. I would see elderly black men walking in the streets and I could see they had been abused, walking with a bent over submissive look, but not the women. They walked with their heads held high with pride and dignity.

The beautiful parks that surrounded the city made it warm and inviting to walk daily as I could not get enough of the beauty, the abundance of flowers, and the lovely, old, elegant homes. The youth had such beauty and confidence and looked as if they could never be defeated.

I took a boat to Angel Island where Nelson Mandela spent 27 years in prison. I was nervous the entire way as I knew all about his life from reading his autobiography. I knew he lived in a 5 by 7 cell for all those years and how he and his fellow cell mates had discovered a way of communicating that the guards could not understand, and that is how they were all able to survive. What amazed me when I saw his small cell is how Mr. Mandela was able to do sit ups and push ups on a cement floor every day in that tiny space. The men would sing everyday to keep up their spirits working in the hot sun breaking up rocks.

When I met up with my Buddhist friends Janet and Mike, they took me to a special beach where hundreds of black and white penguins lived. I could not get over how they mingled with the people begging for food. I thought the color of the penguins represented the country of black and white people living together in peace, thanks to Nelson Mandela and all the people who fought for the Black Man to have his country back. It was a memorable day at the beach watching the people, however, I did not see any people of color, so it was clear segregation still existed. I still felt the White Man had control in a very subtle way.

After ten days in Cape Town I wanted to go on a safari in Tanzania and see the amazing wild animals that Africa is famous for. I had seen a film about the Maasai tribe who live in Tanzania, they are supposed to be the tallest people in the world and also great healers. Upon arriving to the airport, immediately I saw this was a very poor country as the floor of the airport was dirt. There were many men hustling me for safaris, one man made a deal with me if I bought a safari from him he would take me to a nice hotel, so I paid the $200. I also had to spend a hundred dollars for a visa. When the anxious man took me to the hotel, he did not even help me with my bag, he fled. The hotel smelled and was horrible with no running water. Seeing naked children playing in the streets without having been washed, I felt sick and sad. It was raining and I was not going to go on a safari in the rain, so the next day I booked my return flight home. That one day and one night cost me $350, but I was so happy to be going home.

Chapter 43, Knee Surgery

Nine months after a horrible fall on October 10, 2012 that had me in constant pain, I was forced to go to the doctor on July 16, 2013. The doctor showed me the X-rays: it was bone on bone, my knee had no cartilage and no tendons. Knee surgery was my only option. I was terrified when the doctor threw this big aluminum ball at me the size of a grapefruit, saying that *this* is what would be going into my knee. I ran out of the doctor's office, too scared to talk. I could not imagine having that huge ball in my knee, though many friends who had the same surgery said it was nothing.

After six weeks of confusion and worry, I decided to make an appointment with Dr. Fuji, a Japanese doctor. I felt I trusted him since I've had contact with Japanese culture through my Buddhist practice and my travels, and found the culture to be very thorough. Up to that point, I still thought my knee surgery meant installing the big titanium ball, but I never discussed this with Dr. Fuji. On September 17, I went in for surgery. After one hour I was out and in the recovery room glad to see Despina and Josefina there waiting for me.

To wake up and not feel my leg was quite shocking—immediately I was in a walker and going to the toilet. I could not get over how quickly my body responded, even though I knew I was full of painkillers. I had lost so much blood the doctor had me stay an extra day. I never had one female nurse, the nurses were all sensitive young men who treated me with great concern and care.

I arrived home and knew my four story house was going to be a big challenge. My walker was to be my only means of transportation. For 8 days I slept upstairs uncomfortably on my couch. I had a nurse come twice a week and a physical therapist once a week. With the help and support of my daughter and Josefina and many friends, I recovered smoothly. My dear neighbor Mila brought me delicious food daily. Visits and calls from friends made my recovery enjoyable.

My challenge each day was the painful work on the range of motion that I lost when the doctor cut my knee in half and installed two small steel joints. This I discovered when my physical therapist came to my home and showed me what my knee replacement looked like. I was shocked that I had been so misinformed by that cold and heartless doctor who, I would find out, had thrown a *hip* joint at me back in July. I immediately filed a complaint against the doctor. I could not believe I had gone through all that painful surgery thinking I had a hip replacement in my knee.

Since I am a very active woman who loves to swim and ride my bicycle, my recovery was excellent. I felt proud of myself every time I went to physical therapy seeing how much I had improved. Sitting in a chair was painful and walking was challenging, but every day I looked for a new challenge to show myself I was improving. Walking down and up 90 stairs in my house was my biggest challenge.

Chapter 44, Gratitude

Now I must write about gratitude since I have written a great deal of my struggle that has made me strong. I want to write about my oldest best friends whom I miss as they now live in Lakeport and I moved to be near them. Ruthie and Judy have been so important in my life. I feel we have known each other for many lifetimes.

It all began back in the 70s when we were all coming out of the closet, the gay liberation was in full swing. It has taken 45 years for it be legal for gays to marry which is quite amazing. In the early 70s, my daughter Despina made me put an ad in the Bay Guardian newspaper to find a new lover as she could not stand my depression after my breakup with whomever it was—there were so many brief encounters. I was naive about life. Since my father had told me my value was sex I gave it away freely. If the sex was not there, I thought it was not a valuable relationship.

My first caller a week after posting the ad was Judy Fine, I immediately loved her warmth and especially her humor. We talked like friends for quite a while, I could not believe my fortune, it was so easy. I never responded to any of the other callers. I did not like the sound of their voices.

Judy and I met a week later and became friends. I introduced her to my Buddhist practice. A few months later I went over to her home. I noticed my name on her altar. I had chanted for Judy's happiness and soon after Judy came to my home with a good looking, lovely, exciting blond woman named Ruthie, who is a Capricorn just like me. Judy is also a lovely good looking black haired woman with sparkling brown eyes, and Ruthie is a little sexy South African woman with dancing blue eyes. I thought immediately that they were lovers, they felt so right together. That was to happen later on, but I recognized that they too were connected in many lives as I have felt this so often with my own ex-lovers that have been the most challenging.

They moved down the street from me and soon I was to find out how interesting these two women were together. Their relationship has been extremely close. They have excellent communication and they have worked through their issues. Ruthie financed her brother-in-law through Stanford University, he has become quite rich and has taken care of them both to this day.

I miss my friends because we were so close—even if we did not see each often, we were close. I would not have what I call my tree house if it had not been for them. They have been there for me in all my difficult relations, they really understand people and the matters of the heart. They make friends quite easily as they understand appreciation, giving of themselves all the time.

Sadly, their neighbor in Healdsburg built a vineyard right next to their house and the spray they put on the grapes made them both ill, they had to move to Lakeport in Lake County where I had the fortune to spend summers in the town of Nice which is close to Lakeport. Every time I visit them I feel like I am returning to my wonderful childhood.

Chapter 45, My Loved Ones

My Buddhist practice is what has sustained me for 45 years. I know without Nam Myoho Renge Kyo in my head, my fundamental darkness would have driven me to suicide. When I had found my Roxanne dead in her car, I knew if it had not been for my practice I would have easily ended my life.

Zachary, my grandson, has become my mentor. He is such a strong Buddhist because of his karma. Like everyone in our family frightened of life, he too was able to embrace this awesome practice. He has made the impossible possible and was chosen out of thousands of youth to attend the University of California, at Berkeley. He chants an hour every morning and constantly shows me actual proof. As everyone says, he is a Buddha never giving into his negativity. I have suffered so much in all my relationships and he is the one who has told me that I "need to appreciate all my negativity and turn it into a benefit." That needy little kid inside of me is what I am constantly challenged with but he finds a way to always reassure me.

I swim every day for a half an hour and do Qigong breathing exercises, inhaling to the count of five and exhaling to the count of ten. This is done in different positions which has kept my body strong. I want to show actual proof that I can live to be a 100 and be viable and happy. It takes discipline—I have always known that.

When my dear friend Danielle read me Phyllis Vega's astrology book, I heard an astonishingly accurate revelation about me:

> "Those born [on January 3rd] have vibrant, outgoing personalities that make them extremely popular with their many friends and associates. Although you are as hard-working and responsible as any goat, you're also fun loving and sociable. The serious side of your Capricorn nature is lightened by your youthful effervescence and great sense of humor. You are full of enthusiasm and original ideas, but your interest in attempting new things can cause you to spread yourself too thin. People with birthdays on January 3 possess wonderful imaginations and a flair for the dramatic...you are naturally artistic, and [your] love for the limelight are equaled only by your desire for material success. Your fluency with

language and an ease of self-expression guarantees that you're never at a loss for words. You are dependable and determined but nevertheless refuse to let personal responsibilities or career aspirations keep you from having a good time."

Miss Vega gave me a new window of appreciation for my birth sign. At 81, I am finally starting to appreciate myself.

My greatest critic is my daughter Despina as she always makes me see myself in ways that amaze me. She has a great deal of appreciation for me but makes me see when I am full of myself. My significant other, Josefina, loyally continues to fascinate me, as I have not been loyal to her since she too is not that sexual. Why do I always pick non-sexual women? Most of the women I have been with are not that sexual. Sex has always been my focus in intimate romantic relationships but it has finally fazed out of its demand on me.

Josefina occupies a privileged place in my heart and without her my love would have nowhere to go. I would be wandering in limbo as her kindness also continues to amaze me. She is a Leo, a sign with the need to have a position of entitlement. Though Josefina is not financially wealthy, she has an abundance of friends, she is a great listener and has a big heart for all those who are suffering. I shall never forget when we were traveling in Spain and a young man passed out in the street right in front of us, she was ready immediately to give him mouth to mouth respiration. She has become a special member of our family as she is the one who knows how to get a party organized and get dancing the people who thought they could not dance. Her amazing energy at a party is astronomical. She loves to dance and she and her friends all do the same kind of dances which I, as a former dance teacher was never able to do. I have learned humility with Josefina as I have the money and she has the looks and the charm that beholds me to do my human revolution.

I thought I had retired from traveling after 6 years of not wanting to deal with airports and tight seats on planes, but all of a sudden a cheap flight to Mexico City enticed me to go with my daughter to Mexico City in August 2015 to visit Josefina and her incredibly large family.

I wanted to visit our new huge Buddhist Cultural Center in Mexico City. Our sect of Buddhism has spread to over 192 countries and territories with millions of members all over the world. We are the Soka Gakkai, which means value-creating society. Our goal is

Kosen-rufu, roughly translated to world peace, as which my mentor Daisaku Ikeda describes, "Kosen-rufu is nothing other than building an age of spiritual revolution where each person acts based on a deep belief in the infinitely noble Buddha nature inherent in all people." Greed, anger and stupidity dominate the world and that is why the world is in such a painful situation, which is why we need a transformation in the human heart to change it.

Introducing this practice to people is my greatest joy and to have many new members in my district here in Healdsburg is awesome. Especially Deborah Sutter who I introduced to this practice 27 years ago before we lost contact. All of a sudden she found my daughter on Facebook and now she and her lover Lo are practicing here in Healdsburg. It seems when we lose contact with someone we love and then find them, we appreciate them more.

At my age of 81, people are passing on to their next life—last month three people went to the other side which shocked me. First was Betty Guy, who I have called Liz in my earlier chapters, and whose death began a month of crying and missing her like I had never experienced before. Now, it is like I am having a relationship with her, reliving our wonderful past and the intimacy we shared. She had made it possible for me to finish college, become a teacher, retire and to know how to travel the world. Such a tragedy with a tease of greatness dying inside of me wanting to break out of the shackles of my loss. We would express our feelings so intensely with our bodies crying out for connection after so many lifetimes apart. I know I will see you again my dearest one. I will wait, for life is a collection of memories.

Next Deborah Sutter's mother, Marge, passed as well. I became close to her, she was blind and suffered from diabetes. She lost her sight first, then her two toes, and when the doctors were going to cut off her foot, she said no more and then slowly passed on to her next life. Marge had the same energy that Betty had, a Virgo—we got along wonderfully and I visited her every week. I miss her, we really enjoyed each other.

Two weeks later I heard at an AA meeting that Ana Maria, my former lover, had died of a heart attack. I was relieved with that news that she was no longer in pain because we had a bad ending in our relationship. I understand why in AA they state you should not become emotionally involved with your sponsor. She had helped me become sober though I paid a high price financially.

Being a Buddhist, I know that everything we do is our karma and there is no one else to blame. It took me years to overcome being a victim, which my mother had taught me so well. Recovering from being a Catholic has been the hardest challenge for me. I go to my AA meetings but know it is just for me not to pick up that drink. When my drinking got out of control last year, I knew I had to return to AA. I go to my Monday night meetings every week and what is really great is that I have introduced three AA members to my Buddhist practice. In AA you are supposed to turn it over to your higher power and that does not work for me. Meditating for me is looking at your problems, while chanting Nam Myoho Renge Kyo and looking to the Gohonzon is like a mirror looking into my life and seeing the solution.

My greatest joy is introducing this Buddhist practice to people and watching them do their human revolution and become happy.

Before I end my story, I must write about the most amazing woman I have ever known. Her name is Grecia, I wrote about her briefly in my chapters on Cuba but I want to go into the depth of her greatness and why she is the person I admire the most. First she is alive and a Capricorn like myself. She still lives in Havana, Cuba and even though I met her years ago, I want to tell her story. She was born under the ruthless dictator Batista who robbed the poor to give to the rich. Her father was a doctor and cared about the people. He did make enough money to buy the beautiful house that Grecia still lives in to this day.

Grecia has an abundance of warmth and affection and her smile is totally engaging. She was the only child of this special couple who loved the revolution of 1950. Grecia was 13 at that time and she knew she wanted to be a teacher so she volunteered to go into the mountains and teach the people how to read, it was called *alfabetización*. Castro created this so everybody could learn how to read; before the revolution only the rich youth could go to school. Castro followed his mentor Jose Marti, who was known as the "Apostle of the Cuban Revolution." As Marti said, "The only truth and the only force in this life is love." He is the one who wanted every Cuban to know how to read and believed everyone should be able to write their own story. Grecia was actual proof of this man as she became a professor of chemistry at the University of Havana and on Saturdays she would do private tutoring for her struggling students. I visited schools in Cuba and was amazed at how bright the students were, they were full of questions.

Grecia married the man she adored and had a gorgeous son with him, then the world of greed entered their life and Cesar wanted to go to the U.S. to make money. He was a pure capitalist and left Grecia with the hope that he would send for her. Well, when he got to Miami he met another woman and married her so he could stay in the U.S. This did not stop Grecia from loving him—she had pictures all over her bedroom of him, even though she had a lover living with her. Grecia would tell me, "Someday Cesar will return to me." She really believed this. Her son Ahmed is a gorgeous young man with tattoos all over his body. Grecia grows an abundance of herbs in her garden along with other vegetables. Grecia was a strong member of the Communist party and fought along with Castro for the freedom of Cuba.

What impressed me is that the Catholic Church in Cuba is like a museum: there is no one practicing so when I introduced her to Buddhism she was happy. There were only a very few practicing members of the SGI in Cuba thirteen years ago when I first went, and now there are a thousand people practicing.

What is most amazing is that last year her husband was in accident that made him not able to stand on his left leg so he received $500 a month for the rest of his life. After that he returned to Cuba and into the loving arms of Grecia. She always said he would return, her only sadness is that her son is now in the U.S. making good money, but he is fat from all the junk food—he loves to eat. Grecia has five senior citizens living below her in her house and I have never seen a happier group of people. In fact, that was my impression of the people in Cuba: they take care of each other. You always hear people playing music, they are rich with humanity and Grecia is actual proof of this amazing country. What is totally wonderful is that I was able to introduce her to our Buddhist practice and she loves it, introducing many people herself to our practice.

After reading three of Gabriel Garcia Marquez's books, I have been inspired to continue my writing journey, it has been my main creative expression. During the most recent drought in 2016, my writing inspiration dried up with the river. Clouds cast great blue and black colors showering over my tree house here on my beautiful Russian River but there were only light drizzles where the drought made the river look like a creek. Fortunately, the rains have returned and we once again have water which has inspired me to finish my memoir.

Mila, my most outrageous neighbor must be in my story as she is so important in my life. We are the only older women on this twisting, winding Fitch Mountain Road. I was walking down my country road one day, in September 2006. Out of nowhere, I hear this soft sweet voice beckoning me over to her. "Would you like to try a European massage, I would like to give you one." I was quite shocked but pleased with her sincerity and her warmth. I was curious about this Russian couple. I had seen Mila's husband on the road many times and I did not like him as he would never say good morning and he had a sultry, haggard look about him that made me uncomfortable.

The following week I went for my first massage. Mila gave me a massage like I never had before. She is a strong woman who uses her forearms as well as her hands to do deep penetration in tired or tense muscles. After she massages each part of your body, she puts a hot towel on that part to intensify the effect. I never had had a facial before so I was quite pleased with my first one. I asked her, "How much do you charge?" She said for you, $25, I decided I could afford a weekly massage and looked forward to my next visit.

After a month, I went to Mila's home again and I was shocked to see five suitcases outside of her door on the deck. I asked Mila, "What is happening?" She said her husband Vadim was returning to his first wife. I did not ask why. After the massage Mila invited me to dinner the following Sunday. This was to begin a wonderful friendship, Mila was suffering with her husband's leaving her, but she wanted me to be her friend as we were the only two older women on our road.

On my first Sunday night with Mila, she served me the most delicious meal full of variety, starting with her famous borscht then lamb and rice with a variety of spices. She loves to feed her family and friends. I am always given food to take home.

A month later Mila told me she had breast cancer. Of course she smoked two packs of cigarettes a day and was a heavy drinker. She told me she was not going to stop her massage business or inviting me to dinner. When she was to go into surgery, I took her to the hospital at five in the morning. Her family came after that and I did not see her for a couple of weeks. Then she called me to come for a massage. I could not believe she was back at work so soon. She is without a doubt the most powerful woman I have ever met, after having both breasts removed, she was back to work in a month.

I began to ask her questions about her life as I found her fascinating. She recounted how she was born in Moscow, Russia to Jewish parents. It was October 7, 1945, during the reign of Joseph Stalin. Stalin who was terrified of the Jews, persecuted them by kidnapping people in the middle of the night to keep them under his control. Mila was born to Jewish parents who were both middle aged. Her father was 60 and blind, her mother was 50 years old and in poor health. She was basically raised by her older sister. Mila was treated like a little princess—everyone in the family doted on her. She became the pride of her big family, learning to play the piano easily and being an excellent student. Everything she did she excelled.

Poverty was their greatest obstacle. Mila would stand in a line all day for a piece of bread. Going hungry was common which made Mila crave food to this day: she has three refrigerators full of food, and when we go to Costco she goes crazy buying food.

When Mila was in high school, one of her professors fell in love with her. Her parents encouraged her to marry him so she would have a better life. She had her first son Gregory at the age of 18 but continued her education as she wanted to become a doctor. Sasha, her husband, encouraged her. One day coming home from school on the bus, she observed this young handsome man staring at her. She was totally taken with his charm and good looks. She looked forward to seeing him each day on the bus. Eventually they stroke up a friendship and become lovers, secretly. The passion she had with this young man named Dima is something she never had experienced. She stayed in bed with Dima for weeks making passionate love. Dima's mother would bring them food. When she finally returned home to Sasha, he was crazed with anger and jealousy. Mila told him she was in love with Dima. Sasha kicked her out of the house and demanded he raise their son Gregory.

Mila and Dima moved in together, and soon she became pregnant. Dima was not happy about this, but he married Mila after her divorce from Sasha. Dima was an extremely jealous man and caused her a great deal of pain. After being together for five years and giving birth to their love child, they separated. Mila was devastated—she had to raise her son Dima alone, but fortunately as a doctor, she could support herself.

One day, she met an older Russian gentleman who had been living in the U.S. for 40 years, Nick. He was taken with Mila's beauty and youth, and he showered her with gifts from the US. and showed her pictures of his two homes: one in Healdsburg and one in

San Francisco. Mila was taken with his generosity, kindness, and wealth. She had always wanted to come to the U.S. but never thought it could ever happen. Her dream had come true. Nick offered to bring her son Dima, who was now 8 years old and two of her nieces so she would not be lonely.

Mila moved to the U.S. and was very happy, she learned English easily and began to work as a massage therapist. Nick did not like Mila working but he then devoted his life to guiding Dima and taught him many skills and how to be a responsible young man.

After fifteen years, Nick had a severe heart attack and died. In his will, he wanted his best friend Vadim to take care of Mila. This was to lead to the greatest disaster of Mila's life: Vadin had slowly taken out all the equity out of Nick's houses and then Mila lost her restaurant. Besides Vadim was a terrible womanizer. That is when I was to come on the scene. Now Mila must work the rest of her life. The irony of this horror story is now Vadim wants to return to Mila. Thank goodness Mila is finally free.

Chapter 46, My Son in Law is Becoming My Daughter in Law

When I first met Terika, she was known as Ted. In my story this person will be called Ted more often than Terika, but she prefers Terika. The first time my daughter Despina had sex with Ted, she told me she felt he was conflicted. She stopped seeing him because she felt he was a spoiled eastern establishment white boy. Though they met at our Buddhist center, she thought that he had depth and a curious difference from the conventional norms that he was raised by. Then Despina became pregnant after being told that she could not have children. A year after their first son Miles was born, they got back together and Ted moved in with Despina. She had wanted a child, and this was the hook that united them. She did not want to marry Ted though, as she felt he was not available. He was a devoted father and then she became pregnant again when Miles was two and half years old. They were now engaged and Despina decided to marry Ted since he had consistently asked for this.

Ted and Despina had a lovely wedding in our Buddhist temple in Pinole. Miles proudly carried the ring down the aisle. When Zachary was born, Ted showed us all he was a great father, he was totally there for his sons.

Ted used humor as a tool for communication, the three of them love to tell each other jokes. Humor united them. Ted would find books by great comics to share with his sons. There was always a lot of laughter going on in the house while the boys grew up. Ted told me one of his favorite memories is when the boys were young and always arguing in the back seat of the car. As they were coming to a stop sign fifteen yards away, he told the boys "You can swear all the way to the stop sign then you must be quiet." They would scream "shit, fuck, screw" and other bad words they could think of, then after passing the stop sign they had to be quiet the rest of the trip— it always worked, he told me.

After Ted's father died in 2005, he began his transitioning, really around 2010. When the boys moved out in 2012, Ted, who now goes by Terica, began dressing as a woman in her home, and she then was attending a weekly meeting at the LGBT center in San Francisco. After a slow evaluation with the help of a great therapist she started to take hormones—Terica is in her late 50s and she will not have a total transition as she feels it is too drastic at this age.

Living in a neighborhood that is historically black and Latino, and whose culture is not necessarily transgender tolerant, Terica dresses androgynously when leaving the house. As soon as she comes home she puts on her women's clothes.

What is so interesting is that all of the women in Terica's family who live on the east coast have sent her their clothes. She has two closets full of women's clothes and loves to put on outfits, makeup, and paints her fingernails, each one a different color.

Miles and Zachary both acceptingly say "Whatever"—they love their father and she treats them with great respect so the only one who is having a challenging time is my daughter Despina. Despina has come from a divorced childhood and suffered a great deal and does not want Terica to have to leave. She knows having Terica as a roommate can be just as difficult as having her as a partner. Sex is not a problem as Despina feels that has gone its way. Terica is a Gemini—the sign of twins in the zodiac so maybe it is natural for her to want to be whatever she pleases.

Terica is a great tennis player, she goes to the tennis court three times a week. She is strong, strength is not a problem. She puts her long gorgeous blond hair up in a bun inside her baseball cap. All her friends love her and accept whatever she does. Terica is truly a remarkable human being.

San Francisco is the only place in the world where it is possible for transgender people to get hormones and operations without having to pay. There are so many trans people in this city that it fascinates me to walk down the streets of my city, but of course it makes sense since so many great revolutions have occurred in the beautiful city by the Bay, San Francisco.

Chapter 47, Fly Robin, Fly

When Robin flew into my life on that wintry day of November, it was a memorable moment as she reminded me of Betty Guy—she had the same energy and charm. It was at our Healdsburg District meeting, she entered the room and introduced herself in a strong voice so that we were sure to know who she was. I hadn't been exposed to such boldness as this woman possessed in a very long time. She would take center stage at every meeting and I was impressed. We became friends and when she told me she was a Virgo; I was taken as I needed a Virgo friend after recently losing two Virgo friends. Being a Capricorn, Virgos are my most compatible sign. One night I had her over for dinner and she suggested I should permit her to give me one of her unique pressure point massages. Needless to say she was outstanding, I understood why she was trying to get all the members to try her massage.

Robin and I would talk on the phone sharing our lives. We would be at our Buddhist meeting together and I really enjoyed her. In January, a horrible rainstorm forced her from her home and I took her into my home and told her she could stay until she found another place. She became very moody at meetings acting strange, people were not wanting her massages. The district was forced to have a special meeting with the all the leaders and it was decided that Robin was not to come to any of district meetings as people were uncomfortable with her trying to persuade people to have a massage.

Robin was very grateful I had taken her in but I wanted her to find her own place as she was living in my guest room. She said that she could not find any other place for rent and I went along with it but felt on edge when she started a fire in my guest room accidently. I felt I was stuck with her. My dear friends Deb and Lo invited me over for dinner on Super Bowl Sunday. They showed me on the computer the many places for rent that were available. I then knew Robin was not wanting to move out of my home and after the fire I wanted her to leave. She begged to stay and I said okay until the end of January. February arrived and she was still there, and the 30 day limit was coming up where after that you must have a court order to remove someone from your home. All I could do was pray and chant that a miracle would happen. On February 8th, we had a horrible storm with tremendously strong winds blowing a gale. The next morning, Robin come upstairs crying, "We must evacuate this house is going to flood." I said, "I am not leaving I am going down with the ship."

Robin cried out, "You're crazy. I am going to hire a truck and two movers and get the hell out of here." I thought she was just talking, but when I returned three hours later after my memoir class, she had moved out all of her things. I could not believe my miracle, she was gone and I was so relieved and happy.

Then I went down to her room and found an abundance of wine bottles under the bed, while here I was in AA and she knew it. How dare she ignore the no drinking rule. My compassion ended immediately. I saw why my members were concerned for my safety, I was so blind but grateful that the nightmare was finally over. I feel sad for this lost broken soul who blames everyone for her life. What a huge lesson this was for me, now I WONDER WHAT THE NEXT ONE WILL BE....

Chapter 48, The Beginning of Forever

I want to live to be 100 then I want to go on to my next life as a man and become a great dancer and have my own dance company. One of my greatest joys is introducing this Buddhist practice to other people. I love to see them do their human revolution and begin to see they too can make the impossible, possible. One goal as a Buddhist is that if one third of the people of the world know of Buddhism, and one third practice, it will change the energy, that is why introducing people to this practice is so important. We must change this negative energy in this wonderful world. Just by writing this memoir and sharing my Buddhist practice I am contributing to world peace. Nam Myoho Renge Kyo means *Nam* is devotion to, *renge* the law of cause and effect, and *kyo* is through sound vibration.

I hate to end my memoir with the greatest tragedy I have ever experienced and that is the election of Donald Trump. I did not like Hillary Clinton, my man was Bernie Sanders but to see Trump every day on the TV is scary and making me chant more than usual. Everything he stands for is a horror. Climate change denial shows how ignorant he is and his sexist and racist agenda is throwing all the rights we have gained out the window. His Muslim ban and getting rid of immigrants and so much more every day is a constant disaster. After reading Hitler's memoir, "Mein Kemp," I am frightened. Trump is following Hitler's platform which is frightening.

Before I end this journey I must include two frightening experiences that happened this year of 2017. First on February 22, I was in my studio in San Francisco. I had climbed my ladder six feet from the floor and all of a sudden my cell phone rang. I quickly turned around and fell to the floor on my back with such a thud I felt I would never walk again. I screamed like a crazy woman. My daughter Despina came running to my aid, and thanks to her experience with icing, she ran for six ice packs to put them all over me and within a half hour I was able to stand up and walk. Not only was I able to walk, I ran down the stairs and jumped into the car to go to the San Francisco ballet with my grandson Zachary. I had to climb 100 stairs all on my own to get to my seat, adrenalin must have kicked in as I was not in any pain. We saw one of the greatest ballets that I have ever seen called Frankenstein. I could not believe I was not in any pain. After the amazing ballet, I drove 90 miles home to my lovely house on the Russian River, took my sleeping pills and went to sleep. The next day I could hardly get out of bed, the pain was beyond anything I had ever experienced. I could hardly climb the 10 stairs up my living room to kitchen. I called my chiropractor, Dr. Sykes, who has helped me for many years. Dr. Sykes is 82 years old but he has hands that are magical. After visiting him twice a week, doing Qigong breathing exercises daily, swimming 20 laps, and having weekly massages, within five months I had no more pain. At 81 I never thought I could make the impossible possible again!

My next miracle: on October 9th, 2017, gusts of wind stormed into Sonoma County that caused a fire like California had never seen before! Thousands of homes were destroyed and many people died. I awoke to the horrible smell of smoke. I turned on the television and saw the ravaging fires all over the screen. We had to stay inside as the smoke was beyond belief! All I could do was chant Nam Myoho Renge Kyo. I was entrenched in fear as I was sure my house would be affected by the fire since I am surround by trees and dried bushes. I checked on my neighbor Mila and the next day we were told to evacuate our homes. As I departed Healdsburg, the town looked like a bombed out city with no one on the streets and ashes covering the city! I went to my home in San Francisco smelling the smoke the entire way. All I could do was to continue to chant as I was so sure I would lose my sacred sanctuary otherwise known as my home on the Russian River! Six days later, I was able to return to my home. I could not believe my sanctuary had survived.

Writing my memoir has been going on for 24 years. Now I must end this edition and go on with my life maybe having the fortune to write another interesting story before I die.

Finding Lidia Yuknavitch's book *The Chronology of Water* blew my mind. Her focus on us being misfits if we feel we are different and after reading her book twice, I realize yes I am definitely a misfit. My fear of men and the sexual abuse places me into the misfit department. Lidia has made me aware that we are warriors and should be proud to be a misfit. How could I fit into the world if I was raised to think that my value was sex? Sex became my addiction and obsession, which made me look for unavailable people as my sex drive was all that ruled me. Lidia encourages all us misfits to write our story and so I have accomplished this and I hope other misfits join me. If it wasn't for my Buddhist practice, where I have learned to make the impossible possible, I would never have been able to complete this journey that has taken 24 years.

Betty Guy during our trip to Europe

A lover and me

MURAL OF ROSA PARKS AND DAISAKU IKEDA
AT THE INTERNATIONAL STUDIES ACADEMY, SAN FRANCISCO

Me with Mom and Dad

At my niece's wedding about a week after Roxanne died, a painful time but a joyful occasion—my smile is actual proof of the power of my Buddhist practice

Despina and Ted

Buddhist meeting in Cuba

Ahmed and his full body tattoos

Lorraine,
Karen,
Irene,
Dottie, and
me with
family

Josefina
and me
in Cuba

Josefina (center), her mother (right), and cousin (left)

Despina with Miles and Zak four months after Roxanne died. The boys kept us focused on LIFE!

Despina with Miles in his first suit for his prom. A prom was something Despina never went to when she was in high school.

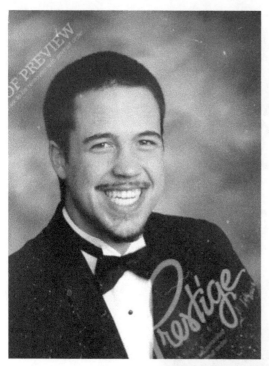

Miles

Zachary

CPSIA information can be obtained
at www.ICGtesting.com
Printed in the USA
BVHW041551101122
651674BV00003B/107

9 781974 484355